REVERSING THE CULTURE OF WASTE

50 Best Practices for Achieving Process Excellence

About The Authors

Lee R. Pollock, former Senior Vice President of Air Academy Associates, has more than thirty-five years of experience in private industry and with the Federal government. Since 2000, he has taught and mentored Knowledge Based Management principles worldwide to thousands of executives, managers, trainers and practitioners. Lee's primary interest has been in developing customized process improvement programs to best support an organization's business plan. The clients he has worked with span the full spectrum of industries and include such companies as: AAI Corporation, Apogee Enterprises, Assiniboine Credit Union, Biovail, Bombardier, Brunswick, Diebold, Ecolab, EMC, Energizer, Gates Rubber, GlaxoSmithKline, Holley Performance, Katy Industries, KLA Tencor, Lockheed Martin, Lydall, MKS Instruments, Morton Welding, Niagara Lasalle, Nova Chemicals, Packaging Dynamics, Patheon, Perkin Elmer, Raytheon, Research in Motion, Singer/SVP Worldwide, Sony, Stanadyne, Stant Schrader, Thilmany, Trico Products, Ventana, the U.S. Army and the U.S. Air Force. Lee earned a BS degree from the United States Military Academy, an MS degree in Engineering from Northeastern University and a doctorate in Operations Research from Florida Institute of Technology. He has co-authored *Knowledge Based Management* and *Lean Six Sigma: A Tools Guide*.

Mark J. Kiemele, President and Co-founder of Air Academy Associates, has more than 30 years of teaching, consulting, and coaching experience. Having trained, consulted, or mentored more than 30,000 leaders, scientists, engineers, managers, trainers, practitioners, and college students from more than 20 countries, he is world-renowned for his Knowledge Based KISS (Keep It Simple Statistically) approach to engaging practitioners in applying performance improvement methods. Mark earned a B.S. and M.S. in Mathematics from North Dakota State University and a Ph.D. in Computer Science from Texas A&M University. Dr. Kiemele has been involved in the origin and evolution of Six Sigma, as he trained the first Six Sigma Black Belts at the Six Sigma Research Institute at Motorola. He has helped deploy and implement performance improvement initiatives at more than 80 companies worldwide. In addition to many published papers and articles, he has co-authored the books *Basic Statistics: Tools for Continuous Improvement; Knowledge Based Management; Applied Modeling and Simulation: an Integrated Approach to Development and Operation; Network Modeling, Simulation, and Analysis; Lean Six Sigma: A Tools Guide;* and *Design for Six Sigma: The Tool Guide for Practitioners.* He is also the editor of the text *Understanding Industrial Designed Experiments.*

Other Texts By Air Academy Associates

Knowledge Based Management, A Systematic Approach to Enhanced Business Performance and Structured Innovation

2nd Edition, ISBN-10: 1-880156-08-3 and ISBN-13: 978-1-880156-08-7 by Mark J. Kiemele, Richard C. Murrow and Lee R. Pollock

This text focuses on the simple but fundamental concept that the right kind of knowledge delivers performance improvement and enhances decision-making. It provides readers with the best available strategies and methods to help their organizations become and remain competitive. The emphasis is on learning how to gain knowledge about processes, products, and people to enable:

- The delivery of value to customers
- Enhancement of the top and bottom lines of the business
- Building of intellectual capital
- Moving the culture to one of structured innovation

The Questions Leaders Need to Answer and Questions Leaders Need to Ask provide a framework for defining the customer need, identifying the method to meet the need, and successfully applying the method to satisfy the need. New chapters are devoted to Lean Six Sigma and Design for Six Sigma as they represent the best knowledge generating strategies available today. The final chapter introduces Air Academy's Competitive Excellence model and shows why a systematic and simple approach to innovation is necessary for the sustained economic viability of any enterprise.

Lean Six Sigma: A Tools Guide

2nd Edition, ISBN 1-880156-07-5 by Murray Adams, Mark Kiemele, Lee Pollock and Tom Quan

The Tools Guide is an easy-to-use reference guide for practitioners who are interested in improving the way they do business. It represents a host of Lean Six Sigma tools in the context of the DMAIC process improvement framework.

Both transactional and manufacturing applications of the tools are presented. It presents Lean and Six Sigma as a synergistic force rather than two competing initiatives. This handbook was written for anyone involved in process improvement, including those who may not have received formal training in Lean or Six Sigma, a college degree or a background in statistics.

Design for Six Sigma: The Tool Guide for Practitioners
ISBN 978-0-9818119-1-8 by Lisa A. Reagan and Mark J. Kiemele

Whether you are just starting your DFSS journey or you are a seasoned practitioner, this book will be useful in many ways. While in training, the book is an encyclopedia of many of the tools you'll study. Beyond the classroom it's a helpful refresher as you apply the DFSS process. The front and back inside covers provide a handy DFSS tools usage matrix that maps tools to tasks within the DFSS Identify > Design > Optimize > Validate (IDOV) process. Readers will learn the IDOV methodology along with the important milestones and tollgate questions, read comprehensive descriptions of key DFSS tools and find out why each tool is important and how and where it is used. The text will also sharpen their understanding of DFSS tools applications with clear examples and illustrations and provide those tools they will need quickly and easily with multiple cross-references and fold-out matrices.

Basic Statistics: Tools for Continuous Improvement
4th Edition, ISBN 1-880156-06-7 by Mark J. Kiemele, Stephen R. Schmidt and Ronald J. Berdine

This text provides a refreshingly new approach to applying statistical tools for moving up the performance improvement ladder. Emphasis is on "statistical thinking" for transforming data into information, plus applications. Topics include: Why Statistics; Steps Before Collecting Data; Descriptive Statistics; Probability Distributions; Confidence Intervals; Hypothesis Testing; Analysis of Variance; Regression; Design of Experiments; Statistical Process Control; Gage Capability; Multivariate Charts; Reliability; and Quality Function Deployment. More than 65 examples and case studies contributed by more than 10 industrial practitioners, span manufacturing, service, software, government, and the health care industries. Included is a user-friendly student version statistical application package, SPC KISS.

Understanding Industrial Designed Experiments

4th Edition, ISBN 1-880156-03-2 by Stephen R. Schmidt and Robert G. Launsby.

This is an applications oriented text that blends the competing Taguchi, Shainin and classical approaches to designed experiments into a new and powerful approach for gaining knowledge. Rules of Thumb are emphasized to enable the reader to implement the techniques without being encumbered with mathematical complexity. Topics include: Full and Fractional Factorials, Plackett-Burman, Box-Behnken, Central Composite, D-optimal, Mixture, Nested and Robust Designs. Included are over 300 pages of actual industrial case studies from a wide variety of industries. A student version of a simple Design of Experiments (DOE) software package is also included.

To purchase any of these texts, please visit the Six Sigma Products Group, Inc. website at www.sixsigmaproductsgroup.com.

Reversing the Culture of Waste

Best Practices
for
Achieving Process Excellence

Lee R. Pollock, Ph.D.
Mark J. Kiemele, Ph.D.

Simplify, Perfect, Innovate

Library of Congress Catalog Card Number: 2011912697

ISBN: 978-1-880156-09-4

Printed in the United States of America

Distributed by:

Six Sigma Products Group, Inc.
1650 Telstar Drive, Suite 110
Colorado Springs, CO 80920

Production:

Fittje Brothers Printing Company
804 Garden of the Gods Road
Colorado Springs, CO 80903

Cover Artwork and Graphics:

Sandia
510 North Tejon Street
Colorado Springs, CO 80903

The authors recognize that perfection is unattainable without continuous improvement. Therefore, we solicit comments as to how to improve this text. To relay your comments or to obtain further information, contact:

Air Academy Associates, LLC
1650 Telstar Drive, Suite 110
Colorado Springs, CO 80920
Phone: (719) 531-0777 – Fax: (719) 531-0778
Email: aaa@airacad.com
Website: www.airacad.com

To Lydia and Carol

Table of Contents

Foreword

Are you achieving the results you expected from your process improvement efforts? Are your customer improvement efforts, cost reductions, revenue gains or productivity realization just okay, versus good or even great? I've seen many organizations that have large gaps between their actual results and their planned performance. Worse yet, they settle for much lower benefits than those they could achieve if they focused on a few key best practices. *Reversing the Culture of Waste: 50 Best Practices for Achieving Process Excellence*, Lee Pollock's and Mark Kiemele's new book, shares the best practices that can make a significant difference in your organization's process improvement efforts.

Process Excellence, as defined by the authors, is the degree of positive influence that an organization's processes have on five key performance measures (or outputs). These five desired outputs are improved customer value, improved intellectual capital, top-line growth, bottom-line growth, and positive cultural change. To be competitively excellent, an organization must perform well in all of these areas. Research over the years has identified 10 key factors (or inputs) that directly impact these five performance measures. In a recent iSixSigma survey, these 10 input factors and their relationships to the five outputs were evaluated (*iSixSigma Magazine*, May/June 2011). An in-depth analysis of this survey data yielded some very interesting, as well as some statistically significant, results. For example, inputs like "Change Management and Cultural Strength" and "Financial and

Implementation Accountability" significantly impacted an organization's success as defined by the five performance measures cited above.

The 10 chapters in this book are aligned to these 10 key input factors, and each chapter discusses useful best practices related to that specific input. I've personally seen some of these practices in action during my years of leading process improvement efforts. I'm sure you have also. What's different about this book is that Lee and Mark systematically organized the best practices they experienced across hundreds of organizations, over more than 25 years of deployments in various industries; and then they mapped them onto the 10 critical factors (or inputs) that are known to influence organizational performance. In essence, these 50 Best Practices provide the "how to" for making each of the 10 key input factors "come alive."

An effective and efficient Process Excellence strategy is needed to assure the best possible outcome for an organization. To really make a difference, however, an organization must identify the tactics and principles for its unique culture, environment and goals. This requires an understanding and thoughtful selection of the appropriate best practices described in this book. Another important point to consider as you study this text is that some best practices may be more important than others, depending on the stage of Process Excellence implementation and the fact that each organization has its own unique culture, mores, values, and traditions.

Whether you are just beginning a Process Excellence implementation, seeking to strengthen a currently successful initiative or looking to revitalize a weakening deployment, the best practices described in this book will help you. Lee and Mark have found that many factors contribute to whether or not a business improvement initiative is successful. There are no panaceas. These best practices represent years of experience, and I believe you will find them very useful in designing or strengthening your strategies and plans. As George Santayana, a 19th century philosopher, once said, "Those who fail to learn the lessons of history are doomed to repeat them." I highly recommend this book to anyone interested in improving his or her approach to business through Process Excellence.

George Maszle
Senior Associate, VP, Business Process Management
Air Academy Associates

George has over 30 years of business experience in various leadership positions aimed at improving organizational effectiveness. He regularly works with organizations to plan and implement large-scale Process Excellence initiatives. Prior to joining Air Academy Associates, he was Vice President of Quality and Business Excellence at Xerox Corporation. While at Xerox, George provided leadership in business improvement across all operations and geographies and was responsible for the alignment of performance plans and strategies. His prior roles also include general management positions, aligning management processes, organizational business assessments and leading process improvement professionals.

Introduction

A general definition of waste used in traditional businesses today is any process, task, step, or activity that does not add or create value for the customer. Who can argue with this definition that has served so well for the many and diverse business improvement initiatives over the years? Is this definition equally applicable to entrepreneurial management and innovation given the extreme uncertainties of today's ultra-competitive business environment?

For mature organizations in any sector, whether for-profit or not, public or private, business or government, the data indicate that – despite best efforts – waste as a percentage of revenue or budget is high. Experience in supporting hundreds of clients worldwide over the past 22 years indicates that 30 to 40 percent of an organization's revenue or a government's budget is pure waste.

In startup ventures – be they small, garage-based, or part of an established organization – new products and services continue to receive a green light based on intuition over facts, taking a huge toll on management and financial investors, not to mention the creative talent and passion of its innovators. Despite the efforts of managers and employees schooled in the latest technical and managerial tools and techniques, waste continues at epic proportions. Though many have been successful in curbing waste, most of our current management styles, rigid organizational structures, systems, and processes still serve to legitimize those activities that comprise waste. Hence, the term *"culture of waste"* is used in this text's title. Waste's infamous partner in crime, variation, exacerbates the impact of waste in any organization. Waste and variation are to businesses today what Bonnie and Clyde were to banks. They steal our money and prevent our customers from coming back. Worse yet, many tend to become enamored with "waste and variation," just like many moviegoers endeared themselves to "Bonnie and Clyde."

Our rationale for writing this text is to share our set of learned and proven Process Excellence principles or "Best Practices" to help you reduce your organization's waste *systematically*. Regardless of your organization's history in process improvement, be it Lean, Six Sigma, Design for Six Sigma, Operational or Competitive Excellence, Business Process Management, Agile, etc., reviewing and implementing these best practices will significantly enhance the prospects for achieving your vision, plan, and passion in support of your customers.

This text is intended for any practitioner of Process Excellence. It should be especially useful for those having operational and/or entrepreneurial responsibility for the organization, regardless of its size, business sector, economic situation, or conditions of uncertainty. The best practices are as relevant to well established, mature organizations as they are for small business startups.

We view Process Excellence not as a program or initiative unto itself, but as a means by which an organization implements its core strategic plan as the figure below indicates:

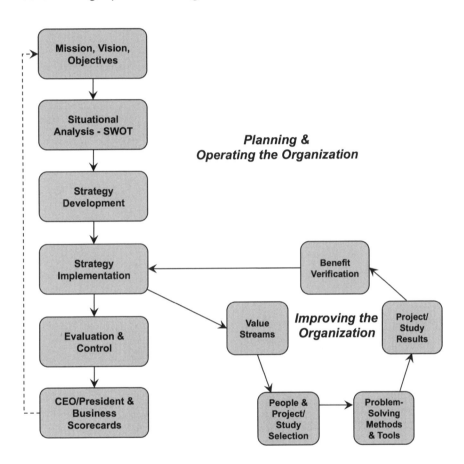

Some readers will associate the term Process Excellence as used herein with Lean, Six Sigma, Lean Six Sigma, Design for Six Sigma, Competitive Excellence, Agile, or any other name that may be used to describe an enterprise-wide improvement strategy. The degree to which Process Excellence contributes to the implementation of the strategic or business plan it supports is a function of how well the best practices contained within this text are considered and implemented. It also determines the amount of waste that is effectively removed from the system.

What are these best practices and how do they map to "Process Excellence?" The expectation from successfully implementing Process Excellence is better products and services delivered faster and at lower cost. The primary vehicle by which this is accomplished is through the use of motivated, properly resourced and accountable, cross-functional project/study teams. These are led by experienced representatives from management called "Champions" and trained practitioners often referred to as "Belts," "Experts," "Agents," etc. The reliance on teams to collect/analyze data and to quickly formulate/implement solutions yields an improved quality of working relationships. These points are illustrated in the dual Input-Process-Output (IPO) diagram shown here:

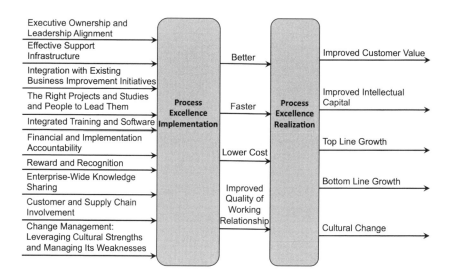

Over time, the expectation is that Process Excellence will become effectively embedded within the organization. Instead of improvement being project or study-based, it should become anchored as a cultural norm, i.e., the way we work. The "realization" of Process Excellence is its positive impact on each of the five benefits indicated on the right side of this IPO diagram. In order to both implement and realize Process Excellence, each of the 10 key inputs on the left side of the dual IPO diagram must be addressed. One chapter in this text will be devoted to each of these 10 inputs; and each chapter/input will be broken down into its associated best practices. Some chapters have more best practices than others, and that is intentional. A master list of best practices organized by chapter is available in Appendix A.

These best practices have been derived from supporting hundreds of clients within every business sector worldwide, as well as organizations within our federal government. Each best practice is not to be considered as an absolute rule. The intention is to offer these for your review and due consideration. As you will soon see, the imperative for some of the best practices is greater than that of others. Depending on the stage of your deployment, your organization's unique culture, and potentially other factors, you may elect to apply some of these best practices but not others.

Though "culture" appears to be tenth on the list of the 10 key drivers for Process Excellence implementation, it is perhaps the most important of them all. In fact, the iSixSigma survey data analysis that George Maszle references in the Foreword confirms that "culture" significantly impacts all five of the outputs. As the noted management guru Peter Drucker once said, "Culture eats change for breakfast." The challenge is to gradually embed the terms, problem-solving methods, and related tools into an organization's culture. Today's "me first" attitude is contrary to this end and will undermine all meaningful efforts for systemic improvement. Constancy of effort for improvement amidst the many distractions and extreme uncertainties that arise over time is key to success.

As you read through this text, remember the core objective: systematically reducing waste through Process Excellence. Carefully consider each best practice and tailor those that make sense for you. This will substantially enhance the likelihood of achieving your vision and successfully executing your plan.

At the end of each chapter is a table summarizing the best practices that impact that particular input. We encourage you to assess the degree of your organization's implementation for each best practice by annotating a score between 0 and 2 next to each best practice. A "0" means "no implementation of that best practice whatsoever," and a "2" means "we do that very well." We encourage the use of integer values for each score, like 0, 1, or 2. However, you may also opt to use a 0.5 or a 1.5 if you believe that this degree of resolution is possible. Then, in Appendix B, transcribe the totals from each of Tables 1-10 and sum. Since the maximum value for each best practice is "2" and there are 50 best practices, the maximum total score is 100. Then locate your total score in the second table contained in Appendix B and find the percentile associated with your score. These percentiles were calculated based on 545 respondents who participated in the Air Academy Associates/iSixSigma Survey performed in 2011. Your percentile compares your organization's overall score against those organizations represented by the 545 respondents who also rated these 10 inputs.

We wish you every success in your journey to reduce waste through a disciplined, knowledgeable, and accountable journey in Process Excellence.

Lee Pollock and Mark Kiemele

Acknowledgments

The authors wish to thank the many clients that we have been privileged to serve at Air Academy Associates since our inception in 1990. The origin of these best practices goes back to these valued relationships that were always predicated on mutual trust, openness, appreciation, and respect. The overarching goal was always focused on supporting our client's vision and business plan and helping them become successful. We fully realize that we can be successful only if our clients are successful. While we are no longer directly engaged with some of these clients, the relationships endure for which we shall forever remain grateful.

We also wish to acknowledge the following contributors who generously offered to read through drafts of this text and offer their critical suggestions and comments. Your perspectives and experiences contributed greatly to the content and your positive attitudes remain genuinely admired.

- Rich P. Boucher – IT Lean Six Sigma Deployment Lead/Master Black Belt – EMC Corporation
- Susan D. Darby – President – Six Sigma Products Group
- Russell W. Ford – President and CEO – ClearEdge Power
- Roger Hart – Former Director of Six Sigma Deployment at Sony Electronics and author/inventor of the *Pivotal Swing*™
- Russell Huffer – CEO – Apogee Enterprises, Inc.
- Dr. Neal A. Mackertich – Engineering Fellow and Founder of the Raytheon Six Sigma Institute – The Raytheon Company
- George Maszle – Senior Associate, VP, Business Process Management – Air Academy Associates
- Dr. Richard C. Murrow – CEO – Air Academy Associates
- Tom Quan – Director of Engineering – Apotex, Inc.

- Lisa Reagan – Senior Associate – Air Academy Associates
- Kathi A. Swagerty – Strategic Campaign Director – Air Academy Associates

Special thanks go to the cadre of world-class consultants at Air Academy Associates. You support the diverse and numerous needs of our clients with extraordinary experience, attention-to-detail, high energy, passion, and humility despite the long hours and accompanying sacrifices with your families.

Thanks, as well, to our dedicated staff in Colorado Springs, CO; Scottsdale, AZ; Rochester, NY; Sylvania, OH; and Toronto, ON. You always make the complex look easy and provide constant encouragement for us to press ahead.

Chapter 1

Executive Ownership and Leadership Alignment

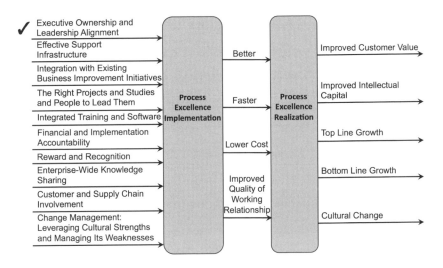

"Bring everyone to the table, commit to a vision and relentlessly pursue its implementation."

Alan Mulally
CEO and President of the Ford Motor Company

Best Practice

Establish ownership at the executive level.

Long-term executive ownership and accountability represents the single, most important driver and our first of 50 "best practices" for increasing the likelihood of success for Process Excellence. It does not assure a successful outcome, but certainly enhances the likelihood of it. How such ownership is externally manifested is a function of the CEO or President's unique leadership style. It is also influenced by other competing business priorities driven by the direction of the board, customer and societal needs, the state of the business and the economy, and a need for innovation.

Before presenting specific suggestions for fostering this ownership of and accountability for Process Excellence, several precautionary notes are appropriate. To be a viable and impactful business improvement effort, Process Excellence requires patience, perseverance and continuity of effort. For those executives who may suffer from a "disease of immediacy," this process improvement effort may be the wrong "horse to ride." A quick dose of training followed by lots of projects may well result in activity with little real accomplishment and another "quality funeral" from which we have all suffered at some point in our careers.

Secondly, Process Excellence must be continued even when an economic downturn occurs. Process Excellence represents a proven set of principles, problem-solving methodologies, and tools for improving the products, processes, services, and relationships of any business. As both bottom and top-line growth will occur when Process Excellence is implemented with knowledge, discipline and accountability, the investment in Process Excellence must be maintained despite the ebbs and flows in the economy. Recognition of this commitment must occur at the outset of the rollout.

Thirdly, it is all right to defer the rollout of Process Excellence if the organization is already implementing other improvements of strategic importance. Too many initiatives within the pipeline diminish the ability to complete them in a timely manner. Often the same "go-to" people are involved. Their efforts become diluted and frustration will result. Implement Process Excellence when the time is right.

Finally, a CEO and President must create advocacy for this worthy effort that will transcend his or her leadership. Though a need for "quick hits" is essential for proof-of-concept and for mobilizing interest and enthusiasm, Process Excellence must eventually become anchored within the organization's culture to become truly effective and impactful. It requires long-term executive advocacy through a succession of leaders, each building upon his or her predecessor's success in Process Excellence. Ensuring this continued advocacy requires careful thought before the rollout begins and throughout its implementation.

What follows next are several suggestions for fostering executive ownership and accountability for Process Excellence. These suggestions are based on the actions of many current and former CEOs who were successful in implementing impactful change through Process Excellence. Many of these are elaborated on later in this text.

Strategic suggestions:

- Formulate and communicate a Process Excellence statement of need, vision, implementation plan and set of management and employee expectations and remain involved in their implementation. (Best Practice No. 2)
- Participate in Process Excellence-related leadership training. (Best Practice No. 3)
- Be aware of and engage in the process of identifying projects and studies of importance to the business using a business diagnosis, baseline, assessment, etc. and continually assess their status over time. (Best Practice Nos. 13, 14, 28 and 31)
- Link management compensation to personal involvement in Process Excellence. (Best Practice No. 4)
- Budget for and create an effective Process Excellence-related infrastructure. (Best Practice Nos. 6-11)

Tactical Suggestions:

- Integrate Process Excellence messaging in your everyday correspondence and encourage your direct reports to do so, as well. This is particularly crucial throughout the first year of your deployment.
- Answer the "Questions Leaders Must Answer" found in the *Knowledge Based Management* book described at the beginning of this text. These questions gauge your

readiness to be personally involved and committed to Process Excellence. Insist that your management also answer the questions.

- Ask the "Questions Leaders Must Ask" also found in the aforementioned *Knowledge Based Management* text. These questions drive fact versus opinion-based decision-making and "pull" the use of Process Excellence principles, problem-solving methodologies, and the tools that convert data into information and information into knowledge. Insist that your management also ask these questions.
- Personally intervene in all "critical" Process Excellence-related events. By "critical" we mean any key event that, if ignored, will seriously jeopardize the credibility of your Process Excellence implementation. Such events are inevitable and should be very few in number.
- Participate in Process Excellence-related training events. Align your calendar with the scheduling of such events and visit them even if it requires a video-teleconference linkup or teleconference.
- Actively seek both formal and informal feedback regarding Process Excellence. Your staff may be insulating you from what is really happening and not happening. (Best Practice No. 5)
- Thank those project, study, and kaizen teams that succeed regardless of the size of the benefit that team contributes to the business. (Best Practice No. 44)
- Remain enthusiastic about your organization's progress on Process Excellence-related projects, studies, and kaizens.
- Communicate success at all events ranging from employee "all-hands" meetings, customer and supplier events, board and shareholder meetings, etc.

These suggestions are not intended to be prescriptive or exhaustive. Individual leadership style impacts how the suggestions might be deployed. The objective is to demonstrate and communicate, up front, genuine ownership of and accountability for Process Excellence.

Best Practice

Develop and communicate the need, vision, and plan.

When an executive-level decision is made to invest in Process Excellence, key to the success of the deployment is clearly articulating to the employees within the organization the need for the business to go in that direction. It matters not whether the business is a market leader or a company in dire straits, for the individuals within the organization the need must be expressed in order to rally support. Until the need is understood, employees will be hesitant to personalize their commitment and level of involvement.

Once the need is clarified, leadership should craft the vision of the future for the company. Is the vision to become the market leader in a specific product or service? Is it to open overseas markets and compete globally? Is it to become No. 1 in customer satisfaction? Is it to improve the efficiency and effectiveness of processes so that the company can compete in a very demanding and competitive market place? The vision establishes the "line in the sand." It should be succinct and relevant, and it should enable the workforce to rally behind the vision through each member's identification of the role that he or she can play in the implementation of Process Excellence.

Once the vision has been created, the plan for how to achieve that vision must be crafted. Creating a shared vision and plan represents a joint responsibility of the executive and the leadership team. The plan should be sufficiently thorough to identify key high-level tasks as well as who is primarily responsible for accomplishing each task and by when. As with any effective project management plan, this plan must logically sequence key Process Excellence tasks and promote accountability for correct implementation. Key elements within the plan should include training, certification, project and study execution, attainment of self-sustainability, benefit realization, etc. The plan should be designed with the expectation that it will evolve over time as appropriate. It should include activities that measure actual versus estimated benefits as well as activities that assess the overall impact that Process Excellence has on the business. This latter point is further explained in Best Practice No. 29.

By establishing the need, providing a vision of where the company will go with Process Excellence, and putting structure to the plan for how to effectively roll out Process Excellence, the deployment will be off to a great start.

Best Practice

Train leadership first.

Once a decision is made to launch Process Excellence, a leadership session should be conducted that includes the CEO/President and his or her leadership team. The objectives of such a session are to educate each participant on:

- The organization's need, vision, plan, and expectations from Process Excellence.
- The infrastructure required for supporting Process Excellence.
- The key problem-solving methodologies like Define > Measure > Analyze > Improve > Control (DMAIC), Identify > Define > Optimize > Validate (IDOV), etc.
- What the "soft" and "hard" tools are, how each is properly used, and practical examples to reinforce each.
- Criteria for selecting the initial Process Excellence projects and studies.
- What the initial projects and/or studies will be, how they will be implemented, by whom, and by when.

We recommend that the CEO/President introduce the session and its objectives as well as re-communicate the need, vision, high-level plan, and expectations. The CFO or equivalent should present the rules for allowable benefits, the process for estimating, verifying and assimilating benefits from project and study teams, and how the finance organization will support these efforts in the future. All invited participants should clear their calendars for the entire session and actively participate in it. This session serves as a cornerstone for Process Excellence and the key actions that follow.

Our experience with several clients, large and small, has often yielded reluctance in participating at such executive sessions. Then, as Process Excellence began to ramp-up throughout the organization, those who did not believe they needed to participate experienced "ah-ha" moments which were oftentimes embarrassing. These very same leaders then publicly took a very different, yet important stand in which they demanded all of their direct reports attend such training.

Best Practice

Link compensation to involvement and success.

Anyone who believes that management is generally self-motivated to improve the processes they oversee based on purely altruistic factors may well be naïve. Real process improvement is hard work and often requires a change in management's behavior. Even taking the step of using data rather than relying on opinion or experience often represents a difficult paradigm shift.

Business leaders need to be educated in and participate in fact-based process improvement activities. They must understand DMAIC, IDOV and other improvement methodologies. They need to require the routine use of these tools for improvement and use these very same tools themselves. And at regular business reviews they need to assess the projects and studies that have been commissioned within their purview. Many organizations set numerical goals that are directly or indirectly related to Process Excellence. The leadership should be reviewing progress toward meeting those goals via the projects and studies they commission.

To motivate their demonstrable involvement in these activities, business leaders should have a meaningful portion of their compensation package be a function of Process Excellence successes. Based on our observation of successful deployments, typical Variable Incentive Compensation Plans include between 20 and 40 percent of a business leader's annual bonus as a financial incentive. When developing a monetary incentive program, care must be exercised to word Process Excellence goals to drive the right behavior and not allow "gaming of the system." For example, organizations must steer away from incentives tied to *quantity* and not the *quality* of their projects and studies.

Scott McNealy, founder and former CEO of Sun Microsystems, consistently maintained the perspective that executive leadership was highly "coin operated." He motivated his leadership team by tying their compensation to SUN Sigma results and behavior.

Other forms of recognition of the leadership, similar to that of the Champions and Belts (further addressed in Chapter 7), may be even more important than money and may motivate other leaders and managers to become involved. Intrinsic motivation is always best, but sometimes extrinsic motivation must be used. The culture of the organization is a key factor in determining what the optimal motivational mix should be.

Best Practice

Continuously assess what is working and what is not and adjust.

A passenger taking a flight from Los Angeles to JFK Airport, New York City wants to arrive at the exact destination ... a mile from the desired destination would never do. During the flight of almost 3,000 miles the pilot or autopilot system is continuously making the necessary corrections expected by the passengers to keep the aircraft on course to the planned destination. As with the airplane example, a Process Excellence deployment needs the same level of examination, assessment, and "course correction" to achieve the desired end state. If a business is content to launch their Process Excellence effort and never make necessary adjustments, the desired destination will not be achieved. Assessment is necessary and adjustment is critical.

Assuming that the Need, the Vision, and the Plan have been disseminated through the organization, an assessment can tell us if proper alignment has been achieved and if the culture is accepting the Process Excellence deployment. As an assessment is generally more successful and actionable if it has structure, categories for review might include: leadership commitment, management commitment and involvement, deployment, development, measurement and analysis, implementation, and business results.

For leaders and management to determine the true health of the deployment, assessment feedback has to be accurate and timely – accurate so that the right corrective action can be determined and implemented and timely enough to allow for modifications with real time impact. Feedback can be obtained via interviews, questionnaires, surveys, town hall meetings, "open-door" policy meetings, and informal one-on-ones. The goal is to get honest, constructive feedback that is actionable. Gripe sessions should be avoided. A good source of highly valuable feedback is from those impacted by the Process Excellence deployment (process workers, "Belt" trained individuals, customers, suppliers, etc.).

Those responsible for the Process Excellence deployment should expect to receive the full spectrum of feedback and must be able to filter out pure opinion as they strive to obtain fact. Examples of opinion-based feedback might include: *there's not enough time to do my regular job and now I have additional work because of Process Excellence; leadership is not really behind the effort, it's mostly just talk; this deployment will suffer the same fate as other quality initiatives have in the past; this is the flavor of the month.* Addressing this type of feedback from employees might require managers to up their own level of commitment and involvement. When employees know what is important to "the boss" it becomes important to them.

Other more fact-based feedback which can be validated with data might include: *the projects are taking too long; there is no management support to accomplish the projects; we need more resources; we aren't making real gains that add to the bottom line; and projects are not driving top business indicators.* These concerns should be addressed and sensible adjustments made to the deployment. The adjustments might include: increased leadership involvement; Process Excellence refresher training for management; synchronizing the systems and structures to the deployment; modifications to the type and schedule of training; alterations to the Process Excellence Deployment Team; recommitment; better communication; etc.

Remember the goal. The reason for the deployment hasn't changed, and the need still exists. As in any other type of business deployment, Process Excellence takes a complete business effort to be successful. Recalling President Eisenhower's famous quote: "Plans are nothing; planning means everything." Assessment and adjustment will get you to the desired destination.

Executive Ownership and Leadership Alignment		
No.	Best Practice	Self-Assess Your Degree of Implementation (0-Min, 2-Max)
1.	Establish ownership at the executive level.	
2.	Develop and communicate the need, vision, and plan.	
3.	Train leadership first.	
4.	Link compensation to involvement and success.	
5.	Continuously assess what is working and what is not and adjust.	
	Total (Max = 10):	

Table 1:
Checklist Summary for Chapter 1

Chapter 2

Effective Support Infrastructure

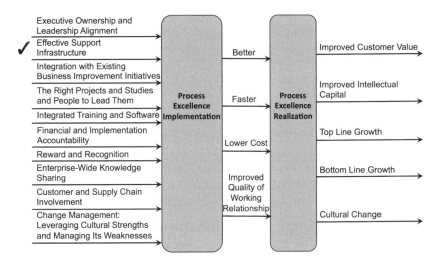

"At times, our own light goes out, and is rekindled by a spark from another person."

Albert Schweitzer
Nobel Peace Prize Winner, Noted Theologian, Philosopher, Physician and Medical Missionary

Best Practice

Designate a well-respected Deployment Champion early.

For optimum deployment benefits, Process Excellence merits the appointment of an individual responsible for the program who reports directly to the CEO/President, reports in to the Executive Leadership Team or sits "at the table" as a key leadership decision maker. This person's full-time responsibility is to facilitate the successful organization-wide implementation of Process Excellence in accordance with the plan laid out by the CEO/President and the leadership team. We recommend that the individual be selected based on the following attributes:

- Highly respected and trusted throughout the organization.
- Knowledgeable of its products, processes, and services.
- Comfortable and experienced in enacting change on a team and individual level.
- Known as a critical thinker who uses data for making decisions.
- Experienced in the use of hard (statistical) and soft (team and interpersonal) tools.
- Proficient communicator with excellent influencing skills.
- Motivated to serve as a full-time corporate Champion for at least two years.

Knowledge and experience in the methodologies and tools associated with Process Excellence are desirable. If lacking in these skills, the Deployment Champion should consider participating in both training and mentoring sessions early in the deployment of Process Excellence. By gaining a competent level of knowledge the person responsible for implementation will be able to help leadership/management prioritize projects that are strategically linked to the business, launch projects, keep projects on track, and successfully bring projects to conclusion.

In addition to facilitating the implementation of the Process Excellence Plan, the corporate-level Deployment Champion should represent the CEO/President on all matters related to Process Excellence on a day-to-day basis. This individual would also provide un-biased, fact-based feedback to the CEO/President on what's working well and specific suggestions for improvement. In essence, this individual will serve as the "eyes and ears" of the CEO/President and leadership team on all matters related to Process Excellence.

We have seen many CEOs/Presidents assign the role of Corporate Process Excellence Champion as an additional responsibility for a vice president or his direct report. The outcome from this arrangement has been consistently suboptimal. Process Excellence merits a dedicated, full-time resource to address program-related issues to include corporate resistance to change; the orchestration of complex projects and studies; the challenge of benefit validation; the diverse requirements for education, training and mentoring, etc. In the end, having the right individual in this role will both narrow the gap between expected and actual benefits and gain much needed credibility with the workforce, customer and supplier base, and the board of directors and shareholders.

Best Practice

Commission and use a guiding coalition.

Once the leadership of the organization completes an introductory session on Process Excellence and initiates the program, many issues and questions will inevitably surface. How are ideas for new projects and studies to be expressed and to whom? How are these ideas to be sorted out and prioritized? Which ideas will result in formal projects or studies? How will the progress of projects or studies be measured over time? How will benefits be tracked against goals? How well are those selected to serve as Process Excellence "Belts," "Agents," or "Experts" faring in applying these new skills to solving real problems? How well is management championing projects and studies within their sphere of influence? Why do some organizations move out faster than others in completing projects and commissioning new ones? Why is the gap between actual and expected benefits so large? When is the right time to jointly sponsor projects with our customers and suppliers? The answers to these and many other questions are important and must be thoughtfully addressed if Process Excellence is to become a viable, long-term effort that delivers real value to the business.

We recommend that a Steering Committee for Process Excellence (or guiding coalition) be chartered to address these and other matters. This coalition should comprise management representatives from operations, manufacturing, finance, engineering/development, sales, marketing, customer/professional services, IT, and HR. Those project or study Champions who have successfully demonstrated the capabilities of Process Excellence could also participate. The Corporate Champion for Process Excellence should chair this committee.

Best Practice

Partner with a capable and reputable service provider.

As business professionals, we are all aware that consultants in any field have varying degrees of professional competency. The field of Process Excellence, which has generated significant numbers of self-trained as well as self-anointed consultants in recent years, is no different. This means that the screening and selection of a provider are critical steps in having a successful deployment.

One of the basic tenets of Process Excellence is to reduce variability. In the selection of a service provider, care should be taken to consider the benefits of using a single service provider versus multiple providers, particularly in multi-national organizations where differences in language, culture, etc., may drive the selection process. Subtle terminology differences often impede the early phase of deploying Process Excellence. It is essential that a common Process Excellence "language," including definitions, terminology, approach, metrics, be used despite internal organizational differences, the international footprint of the business, etc. Though the use of multiple providers is not necessarily a recipe for disaster, variation between organizational deployments within a corporation can create havoc and lead to significant waste.

One factor in selecting a service provider is its value system. Select a provider whose definition of success is based on your organization's success in effectively implementing Process Excellence. No provider can claim success unless its client is successful.

Another important consideration for selecting a service provider is its experience in the full range of required tasks. The provider must have proven competency in the education, training, and motivation of key methods and related tools. It must also have proven expertise in complete implementation, including mentoring/coaching at all levels, project management, and applying all of these to actual problem solving. The service provider must also be a credible, recognized, and respected certifier of those personnel who are deemed to have fulfilled the competency requirements associated with Process Excellence certification.

Though pricing and references are important considerations for selection, attaining self-sustainability without sacrificing competency or momentum is another key factor to consider. Does the service provider have a proven approach and record for helping organizations achieve self-sustainability? Favorable consideration should be given to a provider who encourages self-sustainability and who includes its exit strategy as part of the initial Process Excellence deployment plan.

Finally, exercise diligence and care in selecting the materials and software recommended for use by the service providers under consideration. Are they simple, yet powerful, and capable of being used by employees within your organization who have varying degrees of education? Are the materials, software, texts, and online components fully integrated and consistent? If the materials have been self-developed by the service provider, is an assurance provided that there are no third-party copyright concerns? Is the service provider willing to populate their materials with case studies from your organization as they become available? These and similar questions need to be asked as part of your due diligence in selecting a provider worthy of your trust and business. Often the selection of a service provider is heavily influenced by a single vocal and strong-willed person's opinion or experience. This supplier selection is critical to your organization's success, and the decision should reflect what is best for the organization, not what is best for any one individual.

Once you have selected a service provider, it is important that your organization quickly establish a professional working relationship with the individual approved to serve as your account (or relationship) manager. The client's sharing of key information and the account manager's providing respectful and candid feedback will enable the organization to gain the greatest benefit from the relationship and lead to a more successful Process Excellence deployment.

Best Practice

Integrate key stakeholders into the plan.

Stakeholders are individuals or groups who are affected by or who can impact the Process Excellence deployment and the process improvement efforts that are attempted. They may offer resistance or have issues and concerns in the technical, political, and/or cultural areas. Strategies that enable gaining their support are vital and need to be made a priority.

It may be that the Process Excellence deployment is not met with the desired enthusiasm of all key stakeholders. Process Excellence may require reluctant stakeholders to abandon the status quo and offer their support in word as well as in action. It is important that the leadership and top management team forge ahead as a cohesive unit seeking the vision and obtaining it through the plan.

Middle level managers may see the deployment as affecting their status and "power" within the organization. Some managers may not appreciate the fact that one of their processes is selected for improvement. They may view process improvement as a violation of their area of responsibility. After all, no one wants to "air dirty laundry." Through their involvement in demonstrating "proof of concept," stakeholders will see that the Process Excellence deployment is not only beneficial for the business in general, but it can also help each function, department, and business unit.

At the personal level all need to know "what's in it for me" (WIIFM). They need to know how Process Excellence will impact them, what the expectations are, what role each will play, and how success of the program will benefit them. As stakeholders at any level can hamper or facilitate the deployment of Process Excellence, it is important that each stakeholder be allowed to voice concerns and that their concerns are understood and addressed. Management's willingness to entertain questions and concerns further enables the alignment necessary for successfully executing the overall plan. This can be a painstaking, yet critical process.

In addition to integrating and gaining commitment from all company stakeholders, consideration should also be given to the inclusion and commitment of contracted consultants. They may well be working on matters related to reorganization, downsizing, or even process improvement. Where services similar or complementary to the Process Excellence rollout are being provided by another entity, it is important that the key consultants/players from that entity participate in the training, mentoring, and/or project work associated with Process Excellence. All efforts must be focused on the common goals set forth by the leadership team.

Where outside consultants may be involved in the organization's merger and/or acquisition activities, they should also be well acquainted with the Process Excellence rollout, goals, execution, and benefits. This knowledge will enhance the integration of Process Excellence into any merger or acquisition work.

Best Practice

Create position descriptions that mandate a pull for excellence.

"Improved Intellectual Capital" is one of five stated benefits for realizing Process Excellence as shown in the dual Input-Process-Output diagram presented in the Introduction of this text. This means that Process Excellence practitioners must be skilled in the direct application of the principles and problem-solving methodologies needed to efficiently, effectively, and reliably solve problems that have real and measurable business impact. It is also imperative for the business to maintain high professional standards among this cadre of Process Excellence practitioners. This is often achieved by requiring certification that is discussed in detail in Best Practice No. 24.

It is suggested that new Process Excellence-related position descriptions for full-time practitioners be created. It is also important to amend existing position descriptions for those individuals who will serve as part-time Process Excellence practitioners. Key to this is to align Process Excellence to their existing workload, not on top of it. These changes should be accomplished early on and involve HR, the Corporate Process Excellence Champion, and other appropriate members of the leadership team. It is unreasonable to expect employees to work with diligence on Process Excellence projects, kaizens, and studies while being held accountable to the requirements in their previous position descriptions. This is especially important regarding part-time practitioners often referred to as "Green Belts." For these individuals to succeed, two factors need to be addressed:

- A reassignment of a part of their existing workload to allow for sufficient time to work on and complete their projects, kaizens, and studies on time.
- An assurance that the projects, kaizens, and studies that each is assigned is within their specific work area.

Adhering to the first item above is always a challenge when the organization has already been downsized. But doing so will reduce conflicts between the practitioner's regular job activities and those activities devoted to Process Excellence work. We have often seen part-time practitioners work evenings and weekends on their projects because of insufficient time available during their normal work hours. It is therefore essential to off-load a portion of their work to avoid this conflict and amend their position description accordingly. Of course, the goal should be to align Process Excellence work with the practitioner's daily regimen and eliminate this conflict altogether.

A brief comment on position descriptions for full-time Process Excellence practitioners bears merit. Your organization will have to decide whether or not to back-fill openings created by re-assigning first-tier personnel to work as full-time practitioners. Options include hiring personnel to fill those new vacancies or re-distributing their work to other individuals. The decision may be made on an individual basis rather than deciding entirely on one option or the other. It is important to recognize this as an issue and address it early on – well before the first training activity commences.

If the process for aligning personnel with full and part-time Process Excellence positions proves to be relatively easy, there is something fundamentally wrong with that process. Selecting the right people to execute worthwhile projects, and effectively and efficiently implementing the changes that each project team recommends will be difficult but also rewarding. Management will need to exercise care in selecting the most respected and most experienced promotion-worthy employees to serve as Process Excellence practitioners. These are individuals most likely to already be in key positions throughout the organization. Selecting less qualified individuals will compromise the rollout by introducing higher risk in generating early successes and by enlarging the gap between expected and actual benefits. Remember that "burning out" our best people must never be associated with Process Excellence.

Best Practice

Quickly attain a critical mass of practitioners.

It is important that the deployment plan be well thought out and executed. Timing becomes a critical factor. The goal is to have all levels trained at the appropriate time so that when a project has been selected: (1) it is linked to a strategic objective of the business; (2) it has a Champion who has been appropriately trained and knows his/her role and responsibilities; (3) it has the appropriate Belt level assigned to it; and (4) resources and time have been made available. When these conditions are satisfied, the business has achieved critical mass. In other words, the right level of staffing has occurred; those working the project possess the appropriate level of knowledge; management is involved; and the team possesses the right skill set, tools, and resources to get the job done.

How many Process Excellence practitioners are required and of what type? How long should they serve in this capacity? These are good questions that merit early discussions and decisions by the leadership team. The following general guidelines spanning the first three years of a Process Excellence rollout are offered:

32 | Effective Support Infrastructure

Responsibility	Full/Part Time	Recommended Quantity	Recommended Duration
Corporate Deployment Champion	Full-Time	1 Per Organization	3-4 Years
Business Unit Champions	Part-Time	1 Per Major Business Unit	2-3 Years
Master Black Belts	Full-Time	At least 1 Per Major Business Unit	2-3 Years
Black Belts	Full-Time	1-2% of Total Workforce	2-3 Years
Green Belts	Part-Time	5-10% of Total Workforce	Indefinitely
General Employees	Part-Time	100% of Total Workforce	Indefinitely

Master Black Belts and Black Belts who obtain certification and continually lead post-certification projects that yield independently verifiable and significant benefits to the business merit promotion. This affords these personnel with the opportunity to continue using their Process Excellence experience to influence culture change. The opportunity for promotion also incents others to seek such positions as they become available. When backfilling "Belt" positions, the same criteria for selecting first-tier employees used early in the rollout should continue to be applied. Please refer to Appendix C for additional information on the roles and responsibilities of Belts and other key Process Excellence positions.

For organizations consisting primarily of engineers and scientists working in R&D and new product development, Process Excellence may take on a different name. Design for Six Sigma

(DFSS) is a very commonly used descriptor of this activity. Since the objective of DFSS is to raise the entire organization's level of engineering excellence, we recommend the following long-term goals for such organizations:

- All practitioners should achieve DFSS Green Belt certified status.
- 25% of the practitioners should achieve DFSS Black Belt certified status.
- 2% of the practitioners should achieve DFSS Master Black Belt certified status.

In DFSS, the projects and studies **must** relate directly to the practitioner's daily work. Competency in using DFSS methodologies applied to one's daily regimen is paramount and also a key certification criterion. Competency is defined here as knowing what to use, when to use it, how to use it, and why we are doing this in the first place (i.e., how it relates to the business objectives).

Critical mass in DFSS is defined as the number of certified practitioners needed to reach a self-sustaining capability. These numbers are typically tied to the size of the organization. To reach critical mass for successful self-sustainability, our experience in rolling out DFSS to various engineering organizations leads to the following Rule of Thumb:

- For organizations having up to 100 practitioners, all (100%) need to be DFSS certified according to the percentages shown above.

- For organizations having up to 500 practitioners, at least 70% need to be DFSS certified according to the percentages shown on the previous page.
- For organizations having up to 1,000 practitioners, at least 50% need to be DFSS certified according to the percentages shown on the previous page.
- For organizations having more than 1,000 practitioners, at least 30% need to be DFSS certified according to the percentages shown on the previous page.

Knowing these numbers will allow the organization to determine the cadence or speed of the rollout that will be required to achieve self-sustainability within a given time period such as 3 years, 5 years, etc. If the organization is not capable of handling that cadence from a resource allocation perspective, then the time period to achieve self-sustainability must be adjusted. These recommendations are provided here because most organizations underestimate the resources and effort required to achieve legitimate self-sustainability and the time period needed to get there. Self-sustainability is a key factor in creating a lasting culture change and must be addressed early.

Effective Support Infrastructure		
No.	**Best Practice**	**Self-Assess Your Degree of Implementation (0-Min, 2-Max)**
6.	Designate a well-respected Deployment Champion early.	
7.	Commission and use a guiding coalition.	
8.	Partner with a capable and reputable service provider.	
9.	Integrate key stakeholders into the plan.	
10.	Create position descriptions that mandate a pull for excellence.	
11.	Quickly attain a critical mass of practitioners.	
	Total (Max = 12):	

Table 2:
Checklist Summary for Chapter 2

Chapter 3

Integration With Existing Business Improvement Initiatives

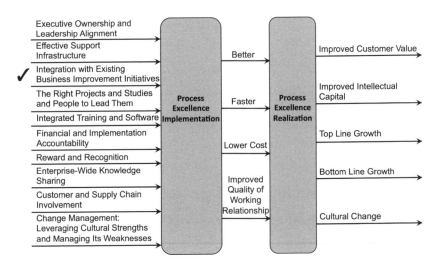

"The secret of joy in work is contained in one word: excellence. To know how to do something well is to enjoy it."

Pearl S. Buck
Noted American Author and Nobel Prize Laureate in Literature

Best Practice

Maximize the synergy of multiple initiatives.

Many organizations have a number of programs in place to improve their products, services, and processes. When considering whether or not to implement Process Excellence, it is important to identify these other programs early on and determine if a synergy exists between each of those efforts and the Process Excellence-related principles, methodologies, tools, and personnel resources. Process Excellence should be viewed as an enabler for other programs. In other words, it is the "how" to get the "what's" done.

One organization we were recently asked to support had a new CEO and President who, after consultation with his staff, decided to implement eight business initiatives worldwide. Once the rollout for all programs was under way, the leadership team decided to implement Process Excellence as well. Although that much program involvement and resource-requiring activity could have resulted in failure due to over-extension, failure did not occur. The leadership team learned that using both part and full-time Process Excellence practitioners to support the projects and program elements that were strategically linked to the business objectives actually benefited all initiatives. With the support of leadership and management, the practitioners were able to prioritize projects, resources, and timetables. Each of the eight initiatives had its own formally commissioned, non-duplicated projects and the resources allocated to support them. Capitalizing on the capability enhancement that is inherent in Process Excellence, each new initiative gained earlier traction and achieved its stated goals. Although this business embarked on a potential road to disaster, it was the Process Excellence deployment that actually prevented the disaster from occurring. Though successful with the simultaneous launch of multiple initiatives, this client's approach is not one that we would recommend for most organizations. It took extraordinary leadership, organization, and management to pull this off.

The Raytheon Company is an example of having successfully integrated Process Excellence (Raytheon Six Sigma) with two other major initiatives: Process Maturity (Capability Maturity Model Integration or CMMI) and Integrated Product Development (IPD). They found that the synergy Process Excellence brought to the other two yielded a renewed and improved new product development process.

Organizations have a limited bandwidth regarding the number of concurrent new programs that can be simultaneously undertaken. If there are too many programs, few if any will succeed, particularly within the defined time constraints and the expected return on investment. It may be appropriate to delay the implementation of Process Excellence until after a portion of the new initiatives is completed. Say "not now" to Process Excellence until other efforts have been reasonably well implemented. There are always more frontiers to conquer than there are first-tier resources to successfully finish them.

Conversely, when you have implemented Process Excellence, use these valuable tools, methods, and personnel resources to support new initiatives. We often hear management vigorously tasking a group or individual to accomplish a new and important task while forgetting to use his or her problem-solving experts who are already trained and motivated to apply their skills on new challenges.

No.	Integration with Existing Business Improvement Initiatives	
	Best Practice	Self-Assess Your Degree of Implementation (0-Min, 2-Max)
12.	Maximize the synergy of multiple initiatives.	
	Total (Max = 2):	

Table 3:
Checklist Summary for Chapter 3

Chapter 4

The Right Projects and Studies and People to Lead Them

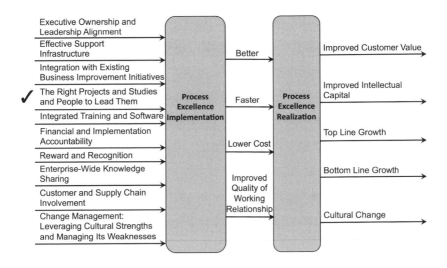

Executive Ownership and Leadership Alignment

Effective Support Infrastructure

Integration with Existing Business Improvement Initiatives

✓ The Right Projects and Studies and People to Lead Them

Integrated Training and Software

Financial and Implementation Accountability

Reward and Recognition

Enterprise-Wide Knowledge Sharing

Customer and Supply Chain Involvement

Change Management: Leveraging Cultural Strengths and Managing Its Weaknesses

Process Excellence Implementation

Better
Faster
Lower Cost
Improved Quality of Working Relationship

Process Excellence Realization

Improved Customer Value

Improved Intellectual Capital

Top Line Growth

Bottom Line Growth

Cultural Change

"Any activity becomes creative when the doer cares about doing it right or doing it better."

John Updike
Pulitzer Price Winning American Novelist, Poet, Short Story Writer, Art Critic and Literary Critic

Best Practice

Establish criteria for project selection and prioritization.

Businesses need a systematic approach to selecting processes for improvement.   Process Excellence promotes the need for measures.   There are measures at the business level that help determine how well the business is performing.   Likewise, each process has output measures that highlight the health of that process.   If chosen wisely, the output measures should link strategically to the business objectives.   Once the leadership participates in a Process Excellence Diagnostic (also referred to as "Business Assessment," "Baseline," etc.) and determines which business measures need to improve, the linkage that each process has to the business measures determines which value streams and processes become candidates for improvement (i.e., projects).   Based upon the performance level of the process output measures, projects can be selected by the leadership/management team.   Once the projects are selected they should be scoped properly so that completing the process improvement project is doable in 2-4 months.   If projects go on much longer than that, the effort may lose momentum and will likely die on the vine due to diminished priority and/or lack of resources.

Process Excellence success is defined not by the number of practitioners trained or the number of projects selected, but rather on the number of projects that are successfully completed within the prescribed amount of time and which deliver value back to the business. Commissioning too many projects, at least initially, will overwhelm your existing operations and people, and management issues will ensue. For the best chance of success, the following guidelines should be considered:

- Project should be selected based upon the measures that link it to business objectives.
- There is no known or preferred solution in advance.
- Improvement is aimed at making a process better, faster, and/or lower in cost.
- Project is focused on business profitability and/or customer value.
- Improvement effort makes use of a roadmap such as DMAIC for focus and discipline.
- Project has a strong business case with clearly defined project goals and measures.
- Project is scoped for completion in 2 to 4 months.
- Data is readily available or easily gathered.
- The project team is adequately trained, coached, and mentored.
- The project team has the resources and management support needed to succeed.
- Tollgates are accomplished at the completion of each phase of the project.
- In new product development, project results may not always be financially quantifiable, but knowledge gain can and should always be measured.

Though the above guidelines are applicable to most environments, each organization will need to formulate its own project selection criteria based on its unique requirements and culture.

Best Practice

Use quick-hitting studies to accelerate results.

This best practice has its origin in the design and development of new products and services (a.k.a. Design for Six Sigma or DFSS). Unlike DMAIC (Define, Measure, Analyze, Improve, and Control) projects that are scoped for completion within 2 to 4 months for Green Belts and 4 to 6 months for Black Belts, DFSS projects can take much longer. For DFSS, we have found that executing "studies" rather than full-blown "projects" has proven to be essential for success. A project is defined as the completion of all of the phases in a new product development phase-gate or tollgate process. That means taking something all the way from concept to commercialization. Depending on the product or service, this set of activities could take up to 12-18 months or even longer. This is too long for leaders to wait for success.

Alternatively, a study is defined as the application of a tool or method that can be completed in a much shorter time period, usually less than a month or two. Studies allow for quick-hitting successes that can be measured and correlated directly with knowledge gain. A study can be the use of a tool or method to answer a question or questions that leaders must ask in each phase of a product development cycle (reference Air Academy Associates' *Knowledge Based Management* text, Chapter 6, for a listing of knowledge-generating questions that leaders must ask).

Examples of a study include developing House of Quality #1 to generate a prioritized list of performance measures; using Design of Experiments (DOE – see Glossary) to develop a transfer function; applying a transfer function to accomplish a robust design study; etc.

Besides being able to accomplish studies much quicker than projects, the practitioner will see that studies align much more directly with one's daily work activity and thus do not become an "additional burden." Gaining knowledge to determine if a tollgate (see Glossary) can be traversed is the real work of practitioners. In other words, studies align much more directly with decision making because of the quickly obtained knowledge they generate.

Studies can also be easily defined via a systems engineering type of requirements flow-down. For example, after system requirements are defined, they are flowed down to specific functional requirements. Functional Analysis System Technique (FAST) diagrams can then be used to drill down to 3 or 4-level deep functions. These detailed functions can then be used to feed a Failure Mode and Effects Analysis (FMEA) that will identify high-risk entities. These high-risk failure modes are ideal for studies and for placing boundaries around the study objectives/scope.

In essence, studies are the equivalent of leaning (see Glossary/Lean) a process improvement effort. They are the quick, single-piece flow equivalent to applying Lean to a manufacturing process. Studies need not be limited to the new product and service development processes. They apply as much to traditional DMAIC activities as to new product and service processes. It is no secret that leaders demand answers to their questions for enabling their decision-making quicker than ever before. The study approach provides a valuable mechanism for achieving that.

Care should be taken not to permit studies to become synonymous with assessments. Process Excellence projects and studies are commissioned to achieve results. The comparison of projects versus studies is pictorially illustrated in the figures below.

For the design of *new* products and services or the *major re-design* of existing ones, a commonly used roadmap is the Identify > Design > Optimize > Validate (IDOV) problem–solving methodology:

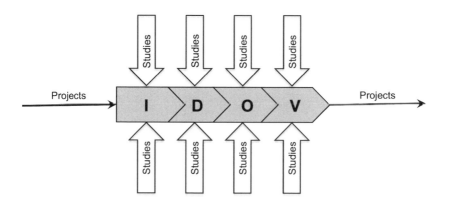

For the improvement of *existing* products and services, a commonly used roadmap is the Define > Measure > Analyze > Improve > Control (DMAIC) problem–solving methodology:

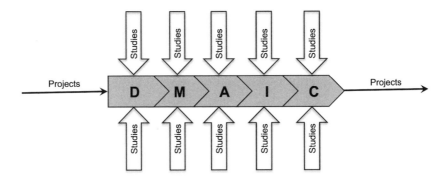

Best Practice

Select top-tier candidates for first waves of training.

Be highly selective when choosing those who will populate your initial waves of training. Your human resources department and its processes need to be closely tied to the selection of your Champions and practitioners who will execute your first projects and studies. These efforts serve as your organization's "proof of concept" for assessing the degree to which Process Excellence can solve core business problems and thus favorably impact your business. If the selection process for your first cadre of practitioners proves to be easy, you have likely not selected the right people. Many managers think, "I am not giving up my best person for some program I know nothing about." Managers must be educated on the entire process, and the question "what's in it for me" (the WIIFM principle) must be addressed. Realizing the benefits of projects in a manager's own area of responsibility goes a long way to satisfying WIIFM.

A manager having tactical oversight and responsibility over the process earmarked for improvement should serve as the project's Champion. The Champion is accountable for the overall success of the project. The Champion is responsible for providing the resources required for the team to succeed as well as for breaking down barriers that will inevitably surface. Champions are also responsible for mobilizing interest in the project and assisting in the implementation of the team's recommendations. Champions are expected to attend Process Excellence training for Champions to help them accomplish these tasks. It is also recommended that they participate in some of the project meetings to remain engaged and cognizant of the team's progress.

The practitioner, often referred to by organizations as a "Belt," "Expert," "Agent," etc., is selected next. This individual will receive highly specialized training in relevant problem-solving methodologies using both hard and soft tools. He or she is expected to manage the day-to-day meetings of their assigned Process Excellence project team. Most of the practitioner's efforts are expected to occur between team meetings, not during such meetings.

Your organization will need to formulate its own selection criteria based on its unique situation, requirements, and culture. The following points illustrate some of the criteria you might consider when selecting practitioners for training:

- Strong written and verbal communication skills.
- Demonstrated influencing skills.
- Willingness to lead teams and resolve conflicts, and able to coach and motivate others.
- Technically competent—is a subject matter expert in an area of specialty—and is familiar with basic Excel® functionality.
- Experienced in good project management skills.
- Has earned the respect of peers and colleagues and is seen as an informal leader.
- Not overwhelmed by simple algebra like $y = 3x + 5$.

- Has the potential to assume more responsibility and become a potential Black Belt candidate.
- Has positive attitude; is adaptable to changes in work environment and actually likes an environment of change; is not intimidated to try new concepts and practices.
- Career potential/leadership succession capability.

The Right Projects and Studies and People to Lead Them		
No.	**Best Practice**	**Self-Assess Your Degree of Implementation (0-Min, 2-Max)**
13.	Establish criteria for project selection and prioritization.	
14.	Use quick-hitting studies to accelerate results.	
15.	Select top-tier candidates for first waves of training.	
Total (Max = 6):		

Table 4:
Checklist Summary for Chapter 4

Chapter 5

Integrated Training and Software

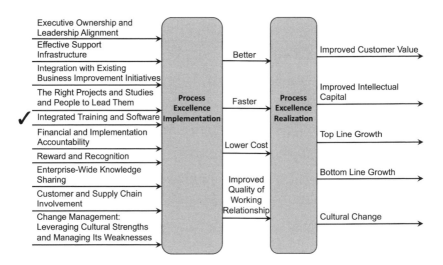

"If you can't explain it simply, you don't understand it well enough."

Albert Einstein
Theoretical Physicist, Nobel Prize Laureate and Author of More Than
300 Scientific Papers and 150 Non-Scientific Works

Best Practice

Use motivational and experienced instructors and coaches.

Identifying an exceptional cadre of experienced and passionate instructors and coaches can be daunting. There are individuals who claim to have the expertise in teaching the principles, problem-solving methodologies, and related tools of Process Excellence. Yet they have had limited personal experience in applying the tools in the proper sequence to generate significant project results. Conversely, there are individuals who are experienced practitioners of the tools but who have limited aptitudes for teaching. It is important for organizations to understand the difference in the two skill sets and use the appropriate individuals for instruction and coaching. Those who are skilled at instruction should be used for training, educating, and motivating individuals to become successful practitioners of Process Excellence. It is always best if the trainer or educator also has practical experience in the application of the methodologies, because that will make the training much more effective and motivational. However, there are outstanding instructors who are unable to effectively coach or mentor practitioners on their projects and studies. Thus, organizations have to develop the capability to do both effectively and efficiently. While some can train and coach very well, most will excel in one area or the other. Regarding the goal of achieving self-sustainability, it is usually achieved first in the coaching area because there are more opportunities to become proficient in that area. It will take longer to develop an outstanding training cadre because of the amount of preparation needed to train and the limited number of replications that each individual is afforded.

Whether your organization uses an internal or external cadre of instructors/coaches or a combination of both, an experienced and passionate instructor/coaching cadre using a proven approach and relevant set of training materials is essential for the success of the projects and studies that ensue. Here are several suggested characteristics for selecting such a cadre:

- Years of demonstrated experience including "hands-on" personal experience in the direct application of problem-solving methods and tools on impactful projects and studies.
- Documented experience in the application of the best ROI-generating tools, including design of experiments, for solving impactful problems.
- Consistent history of positive feedback from previous training and project coaching sessions.
- Certification from an acknowledged, reputable source.
- Attributes of character that foster excellence in the learning process:
  - Skill in teaching and coaching individuals having diverse backgrounds and experience.
  - Passion for the subject matter.
  - Energy to deliver content effectively.
  - Self-confidence.
  - Humility.
  - Patience.
  - Good sense of humor.
  - An ability to inject relevant and interesting stories throughout the training and coaching process to make both more meaningful.
  - Skills in making the complex become simple.

- Gratefulness and respect towards the student throughout the learning process.
- Availability before, during, and after training to assist participants with their projects and studies.

The training philosophy used needs to be well organized and logically sequenced. Go through the material with the instructors beforehand. Does the sequencing of materials make sense? Is there a reason for each topic that will be presented? What are the transitions between topics like? Is there too much material? How will the material relate to the skills and backgrounds of the participants and the culture of your organization overall?

In the context of Process Excellence, an effective training philosophy should include the following elements:

- Well-organized, logically sequenced.
- Regular reviews for reinforcement.
- Adherence to a "present, practice, apply, and review" regimen.
- Use of a Keep It Simple Statistically or KISS approach featuring powerful, simple, and easy to understand rules of thumb to reduce the complexity of the statistics without sacrificing their power for solving problems.
- Integration of the training with timely and accountable project and study execution.
- Continuous incorporation of organizationally specific examples to improve both the relevancy and the learning process overall.

Regarding the specific materials as part of your training, the following are suggested:

- Use fully integrated materials, including guides, texts, and software.

- Evidence of integration within these materials (e.g., consistency of terminology, incorporation of screen shots from software contained within the guides, etc.).
- Evidence that other organizations have successfully used these materials in supporting their projects and studies.
- Assurance that all of the materials are value-added in terms of effective project and study support.
- Ability to modify the materials based on student feedback and your organization's experience in their application.

We have all participated in training events throughout our careers and have developed libraries of texts, guides, and software that have seldom been used. Precious funds have been spent in sending our people to training. When we thumb through the materials from such sessions and realize that their spines indicate little or no use, we again realize that much of the training we participate in only contributes to the organization's cost of poor quality and waste. If you make the effort to select the right cadre of trainers/coaches, using the right training philosophy and set of materials to solve relevant and impactful problems, you will find that the materials are used and re-used often. That is one soft measure of a successful investment in Process Excellence.

Best Practice

Keep the software simple and easy to use.

Process improvement relies on data, and process improvement tools transform that data into information and knowledge. Software represents an essential element in the efficient conversion of data into knowledge for supporting Process Excellence-related projects and studies. When selecting a software package for your organization, consider the following factors:

- The diversity of backgrounds and experience of those who will use the software.
- Ease of use and reuse (consider the learning curve).
- Existing IT systems and software for compatibility and interoperability.
- Use of macros that are compatible with an industry standard for efficient data entry, e.g., Microsoft® Excel®.
- Simplicity and power of graphical images.
- Cost of purchase/licensing.
- Updates.
- Capability of inserting screen shots into both in-class and blended in-class/e-learning.

Many organizations select software that is either too complex for most of their employees to use or takes too long to master unless used on a daily basis. Why pay for a package that has multiple options for doing a simple statistical test? Select the package that is consistent with the philosophy and the written materials used in the training. Many participants will be naturally overwhelmed with the amount of materials presented. The software should simplify the tools presented in the materials and encourage, not discourage, their immediate use on projects and studies. Be prepared to say that "for the few situations where more advanced tools are needed, more advanced software solutions are encouraged and authorized" or words to that effect. Settle on a single software solution that adheres to the aforementioned factors and stick to it with knowledge, discipline, and accountability.

Consideration should also be given to the existing IT systems and software that are already in use in the organization. Will the software be compatible with these? Can the software be centrally hosted or hosted within each participant's computer? How will updates be provided?

Microsoft® Excel® is one standard known by many for efficient data entry. Given both its frequency and relative ease of use, consideration should be given for using a macro that is compatible with Excel® that features the key Process Excellence tools presented in your training.

Finally, consider the simplicity, power, cost of purchase (licensing), and the period for which no-cost software updates are provided. Software is typically an area of gross over-processing, one of the major wastes of Lean. When software has too many features, it automatically becomes too complex. A good Rule of Thumb is that the time devoted to learning the software should not exceed 10% of the entire curriculum time. If it is more than that, there is waste in the process. The authors have found that some organizations confuse Process Excellence with proficiency in the use of complex software. Software should be an enabling tool that accelerates the rate at which you achieve the desired end state. It should be easy to learn and use without requiring daily use to be proficient. It is interesting that some organizations make the decision about what software to buy based on the experience of one or a very few individuals. The decision on software is critical because we have found if only a few people consistently use the Process Excellence software *after* the training, the initiative will not have a culture-changing impact. Recall the mantra: "it's not about you, it's about what's best for the organization."

Best Practice

Use a blended approach to learning.

We are designed to learn from one another with both verbal and visual hints in order to gain and retain new knowledge. With the continued growth of the Internet, e-learning is becoming increasingly popular worldwide. Both teaching and learning, it seems, is now possible anywhere, anytime, by anyone. Relative to Process Excellence, we discourage the exclusive use of e-learning because it limits the human-interaction learning that takes place in team-oriented activities. Some clients have achieved great success with a "blended" approach involving the integration of both in-class and e-learning as complementary and synergistic avenues of learning.

The table on the next page is a brief summary of the pros and cons of each alternative:

Training Alternative	Pros	Cons
In-Class Learning	• Easy to accomplish learn, practice, and review cycles • Direct and immediate feedback from the instructor(s) • Promotes greater real-time interaction • Keeps a scheduled pace for all attendees • Ensures that all objectives receive the proper level of emphasis	• Higher overall cost • Scheduling for max participation requires effort • Some variation in instructor personality
e-Learning	• Lower overall cost • Greater convenience for the user • Greater flexibility based on pace of learning • Higher degree of message standardization • Allows for previews as well as reviews	• More difficult to accomplish learn, practice, and review cycles • Reduced verbal and visual interactions – creates a sense of isolation • Requires greater organizational self-discipline

A blended approach capitalizes on the strengths of both in-class and e-learning. It features the dynamics of in-class learning, including real-time interactions between the participants and the instructor as well as the convenience, flexibility, and standardization that e-learning provides. The opportunity to practice is available in both venues, bringing much added interest and meaning to the learning process.

The blended approach also allows customization. The topics that are most amenable to e-learning can be offered via that route, and the topics most amenable to in-class learning can be addressed in that manner. The overall cost of the blended approach is typically less than the strictly in-class option, due to reduced instructor and travel costs. There are a variety of blended models that have proven successful.

One such model is to use e-learning to introduce the principles, problem-solving methods, and tools related to Process Excellence and to follow that with in-class simulations and exercises that have direct relevance to the business. Because on-the-fly project updates and recommendations are not as easily or as quickly communicated in an e-learning environment as they are in an in-class venue, projects tend to take longer. To avoid this, expert project coaching is highly recommended during the e-learning phase of the blended learning alternative. Coaching will reduce the project cycle time and yield greater and faster benefits to the organization.

Integrated Training and Software		
No.	Best Practice	Self-Assess Your Degree of Implementation (0-Min, 2-Max)
16.	Use motivational and experienced instructors and coaches.	
17.	Keep the software simple and easy to use.	
18.	Use a blended approach to learning.	
Total (Max = 6):		

Table 5:
Checklist Summary for Chapter 5

Chapter 6

Financial and Implementation Accountability

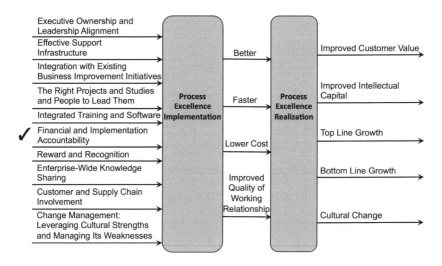

Executive Ownership and Leadership Alignment

Effective Support Infrastructure

Integration with Existing Business Improvement Initiatives

The Right Projects and Studies and People to Lead Them

Integrated Training and Software

✓ Financial and Implementation Accountability

Reward and Recognition

Enterprise-Wide Knowledge Sharing

Customer and Supply Chain Involvement

Change Management: Leveraging Cultural Strengths and Managing Its Weaknesses

Process Excellence Implementation

Better

Faster

Lower Cost

Improved Quality of Working Relationship

Process Excellence Realization

Improved Customer Value

Improved Intellectual Capital

Top Line Growth

Bottom Line Growth

Cultural Change

"Blessed are the young, for they shall inherit the national debt."

Herbert Hoover
31st President of the United States

Best Practice

Use a consistent, simple and straightforward approach.

Regardless of the size of the company, the geographical spread of its operations, or the variety of the products or services that are produced, for a Process Excellence deployment to be successful the approach taken is critical. It is important that a company implement a deployment that reflects consistency in application, training material content and software, level and quality of instruction, capability of coaches and mentors, and commitment of leadership and management. These characteristics are especially critical for global companies, as a deployment can become disjointed and unmanageable if the standards and requirements of the Process Excellence rollout are inconsistent and location-dependent.

Some companies mistakenly believe that their global nature and varying language requirements warrant engaging local vendors even though the approach of the local vendors may be much different from the approach used by the majority of the company's other locations. Another common misconception is that it doesn't matter where the training materials come from and that all materials and software are created equal. If a company has variation in the inputs such as the materials used, the approach and application, the topical coverage and depth of required understanding, etc., there will be variation in the outcome.

Standardization and consistency are the drivers behind a successful company-wide deployment.

If a company has many different locations that reflect a variety of languages, achieving this level of standardization and consistency can be a challenge. But it is an important enough issue to devote the necessary time and effort to determine the approach, the assistance that might be needed from an outsourced entity, the rate of the deployment, etc. Whether it's a department/function that speaks for corporate or a committee (group) composed of members from the main geographical locations that determines the approach that will be taken company-wide, the approach and the rollout plan need to be simple to understand, simple to explain, and simple to follow.

One company that we are familiar with has employees in over 70 countries, and their Process Excellence deployment was very successful. The company determined the approach and methodologies they wanted to deploy globally. After selecting Air Academy Associates, they worked with us to customize the material that would be used in the deployment. As leadership and senior management were fluent in English, as is the case for most global companies, they were trained in English at the level that was appropriate. During the sessions, roles and responsibilities for the deployment were addressed and accepted. A schedule was determined that permitted the management in all countries to receive the appropriate level of management training in English though some locations did utilize translators.

The Belt training was first presented in key English-speaking locations and projects were started. By the sixth month projects were being completed at a healthy rate and proof of concept was validated. Belt candidates who could speak English were then chosen from non-English speaking locations by their managers who had received Champion training. These Belt candidates were sent to regional training centers where they received the appropriate Belt training in English. During and after the training sessions, these candidates, who became Black Belts and eventually Master Black Belts, helped translate the materials into their native language. The translated materials were eventually taught by the Master Black Belts at their "home" locations. By the time the Master Black Belts were teaching in the native language the company was well on its way to becoming self-sustaining and reaping the benefits of being able to more readily benchmark and share lessons-learned across the organization.

Not all companies we have worked with accomplished their deployment in the same manner as the one highlighted here, but our experience with clients has shown that the benefits of using a simple and consistent deployment approach far outweigh any disadvantages. Unfortunately, many companies who start off with a deployment that is not consistent and straightforward are forced during the deployment to make a major mid-course correction.

One of our multi-national clients decided to allow various geographical subsidiaries to pursue their own independent

Process Excellence implementation approach. After the first full-year, the benefits achieved at each of the company's locations were reviewed by senior leadership. The results showed that one major geographical area lagged dramatically behind those benefits achieved by the other major geographical areas. In terms of project return on investment, percent projects started and completed timely, percent post-certification projects completed, decreased cycle times, percent defect reduction...in all areas, there was a noticeable difference. The review indicated that one implementation approach focused on Lean only while the others focused on both Lean and Six Sigma. This difference in approach triggered a number of costly adjustments to re-align the efforts of both.

The key takeaway here is that deployments are more successful if the approach taken is consistent, simple, and straightforward. This best practice, along with Best Practice No. 17 (Keep the Software Simple and Easy to Use), constitute one of the "top five" critical areas for a successful deployment.

Best Practice

Generate successes early and communicate them.

The sooner a business achieves success in Process Excellence, the faster the success stories can be announced. The kinds of rapid improvement events, or RIEs, that we have found very useful in launching and gaining commitment to a program include kaizens, studies, and projects having very narrow scopes. A brief definition of each event type follows.

Kaizen is a Japanese term for continuous improvement, which, in practice, refers to an accelerated team event aimed at rapid incremental change and which applies the DMAIC problem-solving methodology. Kaizens involve some pre-work and some follow-up. The goal is to learn quickly and generate a faster, better result. Commissioning kaizens promotes continuous gains that help keep the Process Excellence momentum alive. The result may not be an optimum process as there is not sufficient time to apply the statistical tools that lead to optimization.

Studies, already addressed in Best Practice No. 14, typically focus on the application of a single tool within a single phase of DMAIC or IDOV. A study may entail completing a measurement system analysis (MSA) within the measurement phase of DMAIC or a designed experiment (DOE) within the improve phase of DMAIC, etc. The goal of a study is to generate a large knowledge gain in a short period of time.

Quick-hitting projects having narrow scopes can step through all five of the DMAIC phases using a pre-determined set of tools. We often refer to this type of RIE as a PF/CE/CNX/SOP event where the linked acronyms represent the prescribed set of tools and the order in which they are used. PF stands for process flow. By mapping out the current state the process is "characterized." Value-added and non-value-added steps are identified; sequencing can be reviewed for logic; potential defects can be highlighted; and sources of variability can be interrogated and studied. CE means cause and effect (also known as a fishbone diagram). It provides a way to identify input and process variables. These variables can cause variation in the output. The entries in the CE diagram are labeled as follows: factors that are currently being controlled or held as constant as possible are labeled with a [C]; factors not being controlled are labeled with an [N], i.e., they are "noise" variables; and those factors that are currently involved in experimentation are labeled with an [X] and are known as eXperimental variables. Standard Operating Procedures (SOPs), along with mistake proofing, are used to change as many [N] factors into [C] factors as possible, thereby improving the process and minimizing the variation.

Once the initial RIEs have been successfully concluded, a combination of formal DMAIC-based projects and RIEs are recommended throughout the rollout. The beauty of any project or

RIE is that they are change events. Without change, improvement will not occur. Each improvement project in and of itself will not change the culture of an organization, but the cumulative effect of many smaller change events can help the organization move in the direction of culture change. Successful projects coupled with the proper level of communication will help create the culture that is capable of achieving the Vision.

Communication, a critical element in a successful deployment, is particularly needed in the early stages. It is important to tout successes, but even reporting lessons learned and less successful outcomes can still have positive results as it will allow leadership/management to make assessments and any needed adjustments. Also, people will realize that the organization is being truthful and that the deployment is important enough to find out what went wrong with those projects that were less successful. People like to and need to be informed about the true status of Process Excellence in their organization.

Practitioners (Belts and team members) who are intimately involved with their own deployment-related tasks probably know why their projects achieved successes, but they may not know about projects occurring in other parts of the business unless there is some mechanism in place to communicate the details to them. Process workers also benefit from knowing about the success stories. Some, who want the deployment to succeed, will be happy for the success and will be encouraged by it, realizing that both the company and the employees will benefit from a successful deployment. Others, who may have been indifferent to the rollout initially, will begin to realize that the deployment is "here to stay" and perhaps, with their support, will be even more successful. A third category of employees, those who initially may have wanted the deployment to fail (i.e., to maintain the status quo), may, after learning of the successes, actually have a change of heart and ponder what role they might play.

There are numerous ways to communicate successes and deployment effectiveness – bulletins, emails, manager meetings, town halls, etc. Some organizations generate a high level of commitment to the deployment by having teams showcase their projects at brown-bag sessions, at business reviews, or at special dinner ceremonies. These events are highly motivating, as everyone likes being on a winning team, not just the team members but also the managers who championed the projects. Giving the participants their day in the sun may mobilize additional interest and involvement, resulting in more victories and making team successes contagious. There is no better motivation for success than success itself.

This best practice, along with Best Practice No. 14 (Use Quick-Hitting Studies to Accelerate Results), constitute one of the "top five" critical areas for a successful deployment.

Best Practice

Plan the service provider's exit strategy.

Most organizations will eventually seek to substitute their own resources for those provided by the Process Excellence service provider(s) at some point in the deployment. The challenge is not only when, but also how. Experienced and customer-focused Process Excellence service providers should commit to and work towards helping their clients attain self-sustainability. Why? Becoming self-sustainable is a strong contributor to, as well as an indicator of, culture change within the organization. The decision to attain self-sustainability and the process for realizing it requires discussion well before the first day of Champion training for the executive team. In fact, the outcome and process should be agreed upon before, embedded within the long-term Process Excellence deployment plan, and ratified at the first Champion training for leaders. And, as the plan is implemented, the process for achieving self-sustainability should be carefully reviewed to ensure the outcome, as desired, is actually being achieved.

Here are several steps to consider for achieving self-sustainability in your process improvement efforts:

- Identify competent, voluntary internal resources to be your future trainers and coaches.
- Transition to certified, experienced, and motivational resources to co-teach and, later on, teach and coach alone.

- Use a credible external body to train and certify your trainers and coaches to the required level of competency.
- Build confidence and provide experience to qualified internal resources by giving them the frequent opportunity to present within the business (newcomer orientations, internal knowledge-exchange sessions, continuation training, business reviews, etc.).

There are exceptions to most every rule and the attainment of early self-sustainability is not different. One of our current clients continues to use Air Academy Associates personnel rather than their trained practitioners even in their tenth year of deployment. The CEO prefers to utilize their Lean Six Sigma Master Black Belts and Black Belts to focus on project execution and benefit realization. His view is that the expense associated with using expert external trainers is eclipsed by the benefits of using their internal experts for completing projects to generate real business impact.

While coaching on projects is more of a continuous process, training is more sporadic. Relief pitchers who do not get the needed reps (a.k.a. work) tend to be ineffective. Likewise, trainers who train only one wave or group of practitioners a year will be less effective than trainers who teach frequently, especially if the trainer is burdened by other full-time job responsibilities and not given adequate time to prepare. To be an effective motivational trainer who not only trains but also educates requires at least six hours of preparation for each hour in the classroom for the trainer's first outing. If the number of training reps per year is minimal (e.g., less than three per year), the preparation time can be enormous. Failure in training leads to poor motivation and disappointing project results. Many organizations fail to understand this phenomenon, and thus what they perceive as cost savings really translates into cost of lost opportunity.

While self-sustainability contributes mightily to culture change, we do not advise trying to reach that goal too early. Using less experienced or ill-prepared resources will yield a poorer outcome in terms of training and the knowledge gained from that training. It will take several learning cycles (e.g., several projects and/or studies and multiple training sessions) for practitioners to become truly self-confident and proficient in training and problem solving skills.

Those practitioners who thrive on challenge and contribute significantly to the progress of Process Excellence are great candidates for becoming Master Black Belts. These experts will subsequently become the trainers and coaches for the development of future practitioners/Belts. With Champions who provide the strategic direction to Master Black Belts and support to the project practitioners, tried and tested training materials that provide the foundation for future training, and leadership that is fully committed and engaged, true self-sustainability is not only attainable, it is highly likely.

Best Practice

Develop internal subject matter experts.

Hiring subject matter experts from the outside is sometimes necessary, but it can also be problematic. Resumes, tests, and even interviews with candidates do not tell the whole story when it comes to a Process Excellence background. One of Air Academy Associates' global clients hired four Black Belts from another company more seasoned in the implementation of Six Sigma. Though the expectation was that the skill sets of these Belts would be advanced and they would be able to "hit the ground running," the cultures of the two companies were extremely different, and it was only a matter of a year or so before the four Belts left our client company.

We strongly encourage our clients to use their organization's existing personnel and develop them into subject matter experts. They appreciate and better understand your organization's people and culture; products and services; and processes and customers. If properly screened and trained, they may more quickly generate benefit to the bottom line than outsiders who may come with a Belt designation but unproven experience and credentials and the inability to integrate into the organization's culture.

To ensure alignment with your Process Excellence rollout strategy, evaluate any self-represented subject matter expert's competency in the terminology, problem-solving methods, and tools before tasking them with critical roles in your deployment. The passage of time and the fact that their training may be sourced to another service provider that emphasized different Process Excellence tools are two aspects of their qualifications that could impact performance. To evaluate competency in the skills that are critical to your deployment, we recommend an online comprehensive knowledge assessment and/or submission of project results or studies that clearly demonstrate the proper application of the Process Excellence tools. Results of the assessment and project review will reveal whether the candidate is ready to task or if his/her participation in the Process Excellence deployment would lead to enhanced performance.

It is important for the success of the Process Excellence deployment that the business obtains a critical mass of Process Excellence subject matter experts (SMEs). Falling shy of critical mass can result in the business losing the necessary momentum. By achieving critical mass, the deployment acquires self-sustaining viability and the capacity to satisfy the strategic goal of Process Excellence optimization.

Best Practice

Manage the expectations of every practitioner.

Process Excellence practitioners in some organizations have been surprised to learn of management's expectations that they include projects and studies as a routine and continuing part of their job responsibilities. Some believed that once they successfully completed a corporate-defined project and certification was attained, their service as a process improvement practitioner was concluded. This belief was particularly true of those serving as part-time practitioners who often are referred to as "Green Belts."

Developing a business culture that thrives on process improvement takes dedication and continuous effort. The rate of development is accelerated when Process Excellence practitioners remain engaged in process improvement efforts well past the minimum number of projects required by the business for the individual to achieve certification. In fact, an excellent measure of the deployment's success is "number of post-certification projects completed per practitioner per year." It is a measure of how the business is continuing to engage those practitioners who are trained and certified. It makes little business sense to spend the time and money to train practitioners only to forfeit their skill set once they complete a project. Continuing projects allow the practitioners to maintain that skill set while contributing to the overall success of the Process Excellence deployment.

It is important that the leadership's expectations of full and part-time practitioners be thoughtfully developed, clearly articulated, and consistently implemented over time. This will help employees decide whether or not to serve as a practitioner and avoid any subsequent misunderstandings. Typical concerns that practitioner candidates have include:

- What is expected of me?
- How is success measured?
- How long will I serve in this capacity?
- What will I do afterwards? Will my former job be available at the end of this assignment?
- How will serving as a Process Excellence practitioner affect my skill set and knowledge of our business and its processes?
- What will happen to me if Process Excellence ends?
- Must I get certified? What if I can't pass the exam?
- What is expected of me after I achieve certification?
- I like the concept of Process Excellence, but do not feel confident to lead teams or give presentations. Can you help me overcome these?

The answers to these and other questions should be addressed before the participant selection process begins and communicated organization-wide as part of the corporate messaging about the Process Excellence program. Management should make it clear that continued application of participant skill sets developed through the Process Excellence program will be expected. Avoidance of the "one and done" syndrome (i.e., completing one project, certifying, and then done) is critical in order for the organization to attain the benefits it expects from the investment in Process Excellence. Continuous improvement is a continuous process.

Best Practice

(24)

Define and use a meaty certification process.

Before stipulating a certification process or standard, leadership will need to decide if certification in Process Excellence is wanted and needed. When our client leaders indicate certification is not needed in their companies, we encourage them to think through that decision carefully. Individuals and project team members work hard and long to achieve meaningful milestones and results, and recognition in the form of acknowledged competency may constitute as meaningful a reward as a financial one.

As we believe that competency is key for those who serve as Process Excellence practitioners, we highly recommend that leadership endorse a "meaty" (i.e., substantive) certification process. The certification standards should require the practitioner's ability to repeatedly, reliably and predictably deliver impactful solutions that solve real business problems. Certification should not be a rubber stamp nor should it be easily attained.

If the leadership approves certification as a goal, then the certification process will need to be defined and communicated to those who wish to consider an assignment in Process Excellence. Certification generally includes the following:

- Completion of all required training.
- Passing scores on competency examinations.
- Completion of one or more projects or studies having a minimum benefit threshold in which the knowledge gained from this training was directly applied.
- Independent verification of the benefit(s) claimed from these projects and studies.
- Successful presentation of the projects or studies to senior management.
- Well-written, case study-like documentation of the projects or studies detailing results and learning, and/or documentation of results in a company-wide knowledge database.

The certification-required benefits can be financial, but they do not always have to be. Financial benefits usually fall into the category of either hard or soft savings. Hard savings impact the bottom line, while soft savings do not impact the bottom line directly. Time savings are typically considered soft since they may not impact the bottom line directly but eventually may do so. The benefit categories should be established very early in the rollout so that everyone knows what constitutes benefits to the organization and targets improvement opportunities accordingly. It is important that, as part of a certification-eligible submission, parties other than the person and/or team who generated the benefits quantify the benefits. This requirement will help maintain the credibility of Process Excellence.

In addition to the requirements referenced above, we also recommend that a certification candidate's skill set should include the ability to communicate, both verbally and in writing. These skills are invaluable when communicating to management and others in the organization the results achieved and how they were obtained.

A goal of 100% certification by all who serve as Process Excellence practitioners is highly recommended, though it may not be achievable. Even with superb selection and meaty certification processes, there will always be some who do not make it successfully through.

The time frame for achieving certification should be limited and made known at the beginning of the Process Excellence rollout. Our suggestion to our clients is that certification should occur within two years of the beginning of practitioner training for both full and part-time practitioners.

An imposed time constraint is important for a number of reasons. It keeps the practitioner focused on a goal: complete the training, complete the testing, finish the project, and complete all the competency requirements. When the individual stays focused and there is a level of accountability, the goals will be achieved. If the individual delays the testing and delays the project completion he/she is more apt to forget many of the tools and techniques that were addressed in the training sessions and instead will focus on a narrower range of tools. Rather than becoming a practitioner with a broad base of skills, he or she becomes narrower in their skill set. Also, the business has invested time and money in the development of the practitioner. By staying focused over a defined period of time, the practitioner's projects are completed in a timely manner and the business receives a return on its investment.

Certification is time tested; most, if not all of our clients have validated it. It is a vital part of the Process Excellence deployment and individual practitioner development. Certification adds accountability to the training process and ensures knowledge transfer, competency, and successful project accomplishment.

Best Practice

Train all areas of the organization.

How much training has your organization provided over the years and what has been the ROI from such investments? Has the training been used to improve the way the organization does business? Have the materials associated with the training enhanced the learning process and served as handy references for the practitioners? We have all asked similar questions about the value of our investment in training. Not applying the knowledge gained represents yet another example of waste that contributes to an organization's cost of poor quality (COPQ).

As with other types of enterprise-wide training, Process Excellence training requires: a cadre of skilled and available trainers, adaptability based on diverse audience needs, and accountability from both the cadre of educators and the employees who participate. When management invests the time and resources to provide Process Excellence training as part of the deployment plan, all areas of the organization should be included. Likewise, all employees should be included because they are directly or indirectly involved in value streams that provide products and/or services to internal and external customers. Successful organizations know that Process Excellence is everybody's business. Consequently, each individual should be offered access to an appropriate level of training in the Process Excellence vernacular, methodologies, and tools used in everyday process improvement.

As mid-level managers are often the process owners and have a natural and vested interest in the processes they oversee, we recommend training these employees early on in the rollout to facilitate their involvement and gain their acceptance of Process Excellence. Alternatively, some organizations emphasize the training of senior management and individual rank and file employees during the early phases of Process Excellence training. The order of training sessions offered and those attending should be based upon the strategic objectives of the business and included in the deployment plan.

We recommend including hands-on projects and studies with all training to facilitate the learning process. Research has clearly indicated that the time between the training and when it is applied to a project is vitally linked to the return on investment (ROI) from training. Tying projects to training also adds personal and professional accountability for those involved and yields earlier benefits to the investing organization.

Best Practice

Apply the training immediately.

Leadership and senior management engaged in Process Excellence should be aware that "application level" learning is key to the success of the deployment. For more information on learning objectives, reference Bloom's Taxonomy. Moving to the application level involves the trained individuals moving beyond understanding what was presented in a classroom environment and becoming practitioners by applying what they have learned to solving problems. They are able to integrate the knowledge into their everyday routines and improve the way work is performed. Using new knowledge and applying the concepts will take the organization to the next level. If the application phase is dismissed or trivialized, the knowledge will not develop into capability and competency. In short order, the newly trained practitioners' skill sets and knowledge of techniques and methodologies will atrophy and the business will lose the potential and capability of valuable deployment assets.

Professor Donald Kirkpatrick at the University of Wisconsin has for decades studied what makes training effective (see Kirkpatrick's Model in Air Academy's *Knowledge Based Management* text). He has shown that the time between learning and the application of that learning is a key indicator of subsequent use of the learning as well as the return on investment (ROI) from the training.

Modern process improvement strategies like Lean Six Sigma integrate nicely the application of the learning with the learning process itself. A tested methodology with a proven track record, PPAR, includes: (1) Present a tool in class, (2) Practice that tool in class, (3) Apply that tool to the project, and (4) Review the results of the application to the project with an instructor or a coach.

To make Process Excellence-related training immediately relevant and applicable, it is recommended that participants arrive on day one of training with a management-approved project contract or charter and Input-Process-Output or IPO diagram. An IPO (or its companion called a SIPOC diagram for Supplier-Input-Process-Output-Customer) is a high-level view of the process earmarked for improvement. Having a contract and IPO will require prep work between the Champion and practitioner before training, but will make the first week of training considerably more relevant and meaningful. It will permit the participant and the management team to scope or refine their project contract and IPO in a manner consistent with the instructor's guidance. It will also promote the immediate use of those tools that are introduced in class.

There are some situations, particularly in new product development, when a long-term, formalized project is not easily defined prior to the training. In such cases, the training is usually geared toward making the practitioner's daily work more productive. The focus is then more on a "study" approach than a "project" approach, as discussed in Best Practice No. 14. In a scenario such as this, it may be more appropriate for the practitioner to learn several tools first, before deciding which one to apply to his or her daily effort.

The goal of training should be to groom the practitioners so that they develop the confidence and competency to enhance the business financially. By quickly applying the practitioners' training to a well-defined project, this goal can be achieved.

Best Practice

Provide expert coaching on all projects and studies.

Everyone needs a lifeline. Even professional athletes who make millions of dollars, like Tiger Woods and Lebron James, have coaches. Employees who undergo training will need out-of-class coaching on their projects or studies. Without expert coaching, especially for practitioners working on their initial projects, the level of success is usually not as great as it could be and the confidence that comes with success is not as significant. Also, projects can lose momentum and direction. With the appropriate level of qualified coaching, DMAIC and IDOV projects stay focused; the phases of each methodology are properly completed and reviewed; the right tools are used correctly; the project remains properly scoped; and the project crosses the finish line on time and within budget.

Coaching must be scheduled on a regular basis. If it isn't on the schedule, it won't get done. Coaching sessions should be scheduled before, during, and after the training. The coaching prior to training is focused on project/study selection and its alignment with organizational goals. It also addresses the time allocation issue and solidifies the team structure to decrease risk and increase probability of success. Coaching during and after training focuses on correctly using the appropriate tools and methodology to execute projects. A simple Rule of Thumb is each individual should have from 1-2 hours of coaching per month for at least six months after commencing the training. While some coaching sessions can be conducted via telecommunications, face-to-face coaching is the preferred approach.

Leaders and managers should use coaching as an accountability mechanism. Practitioners must sign up for coaching, and their project Champions/sponsors, who are ultimately responsible for getting the projects across the finish line, should participate in coaching sessions whenever possible. The attendance of the Champion not only increases the level of accountability felt by the practitioner, but it also provides the Champion a greater understanding of the practitioner skill set that is required and the barriers that have to be overcome to achieve project success.

Expert coaching is one of the Top Five Best Practices for generating project/study success, as well as enhanced return on investment. Unfortunately it is often the least emphasized and, in some companies, is a prime candidate for elimination in order to "save money." These short-term savings typically end up costing dearly in terms of disappointing project results and disappearing long-term financial gains. Results achieved by our clients highlight the fact that coaching, rather than being viewed as an expense, should be seen as a necessary action that actually increases the financial benefit resulting from enhanced project successes. As Super Bowl-winning Coach Tony Dungy says,

"Good coaches guide us and challenge us to be our best. They shape our faith and our lives. Good coaches create good leaders."

Best Practice

Scope projects carefully.

The primary rationale for investing in Process Excellence is to commission and complete impactful projects and studies that deliver value to the organization. Scoping a project properly is a challenge from the outset of the project/study launch through its completion. If not properly scoped in the beginning and monitored throughout the phases of DMAIC/IDOV, the goals of the project/study could become blurred or could expand to the point where the project cannot be successfully completed.

Several years ago, a financial services company contacted Air Academy Associates for assistance on a project related to improving a core process. The company had been engaged in the effort for over 8 months and no improvement had been achieved. It was clear to our consultant that the project was poorly scoped and no improvement was possible because the project team couldn't agree on the problem statement, the goal, and the measure of performance that should be improved. When the core process was evaluated and the problems clearly identified, it was determined that there was no way the original project could be completed in a timely manner at the desired quality level. In fact, the evaluation revealed that instead of one project there should be six properly scoped projects. With leadership and management involvement, each of the six projects was properly scoped, manned, and launched. Four months later, all six projects were completed successfully; all goals were satisfied. In the end, the entire core process was operating efficiently and effectively at the desired quality level. The overall effort took less time and consumed fewer resources than the original unsuccessful attempt, and the return on investment far exceeded expectations. The client acknowledged that the key to the ultimate success of the six projects was proper scoping.

Not only is it important to scope the project carefully from the start, it is equally as critical to make sure that the project remains properly scoped. Due to their enthusiasm to demonstrate mastery and relevance, practitioners often try to apply as many tools as possible on their project. This may serve more as an academic exercise and actually be a detriment to solving the problem. The goal is not to use as many tools as possible but rather to use as few tools as possible to answer the project questions and achieve results. Because it takes more time to deploy the unnecessary tools, practitioners inadvertently permit "scope creep" to occur resulting in an expansion of the start and stop points for their assigned project. In addition, management can contribute to scope creep as they apply pressure to achieve more and more in a shorter period of time.

Project and study duration should be estimated in the project and study contract. Start and stop points and breadth of influence should be specified within each contract. Anticipating a certain level of scope creep early on in the effort, the project Champion and practitioner should plan on de-scoping the effort at least a couple of times during a DMAIC project execution. De-scoping typically occurs in the Define and Measure phases of DMAIC, but it sometimes has to be done as late as the Analyze phase. Project reviews at each phase also aid in the de-scoping activity, adding much needed discipline to the project and yielding timelier completions with earlier benefit realization. As the Champions and practitioners become more experienced and self-confident on projects and/or studies, the ability to properly scope will become more natural.

One way to scope a project or study is to ask what is within the span of control and what is not. This can be accomplished as a team start-up exercise in which an empty picture frame is placed on the floor. The Champion, practitioner (a.k.a. Belt) and team participants – using "Post-It" notes – identify aspects of the project that are within or beyond their control or influence. Those aspects that can be controlled are placed inside the frame. Those that are not are placed outside the frame. The notes are then consolidated and reviewed by all participants as a means for placing boundaries on the project or study before earnest work begins. This "framing" approach is also a good way to do next generation project planning, as it allows a team to see beyond the current project.

There is another tried and tested way to properly scope a project. Process performance measures (located on the right-hand side of the Input-Process-Output diagram) help determine the health of a process. These measures represent what is important to the customer (a.k.a. as Critical-to Customer or Critical-to-Quality) in terms of accuracy, timeliness, and cost. A project that focuses on driving one of these measures to the desired level, while not compromising any of the others, has most likely been scoped properly.

Resources (time, people, and finances) applied to a project are valuable assets, and they should be used wisely. Proper project selection and scoping, vital components of the process improvement effort, will ensure that your Process Excellence team members are devoting their energy to what is most important to your organization.

Best Practice

Establish and follow rules for assessing benefits.

The success of Process Excellence will be measured solely by its contributions to what matters to the business ... does it benefit the customer and/or does it benefit the business? In other words, benefits from projects, kaizens and studies must contribute to one or more key business measures. As the dual IPO diagram presented in the Introduction indicates, the types of benefits derived from such efforts fall into three categories:

- Faster (e.g., a faster process flow, earlier delivery of a product or service)
- Better (e.g., improved process, product or service quality – fewer defects)
- Less Costly (e.g., reduced direct or indirect costs)

Assessing the benefits is not only important throughout the project/study to ensure the maximum benefits are received, it is paramount at two very critical times in the process improvement effort. Each project/study should have an assessment up front to quantify the opportunity. If it is determined that the opportunity is not sufficient, the value of the project/study is in doubt. The other critical assessment time is at the completion of the project/study in order to determine what was actually realized.

Financial benefit is usually the initial impetus for investing in Process Excellence. Projects/studies and kaizens that will deliver "hard" benefits should be the focus, at least for the first year of the Process Excellence rollout. There are always exceptions to this rule, because any project that contributes greatly to customer retention or generation and/or contributes to the top line will be valuable. We must never forget that customers are the source of our revenue. Projects that will yield other "soft" benefits should be commissioned by exception only, after approval by management. Some organizations modify this approach, preferring to implement quick-hitting Lean projects for which benefits quantifiable at the top and bottom lines may be harder to document but which are important "proof-of-concept" projects.

To encourage early benefit realization, it is essential that the rules for allowable savings be defined well before the first project is commissioned. Also, it is important to specify a time horizon when calculating and validating benefits. Typically, businesses will take credit for recurring savings from a process improvement effort for 1-2 years after project completion. After that time period most businesses will have built that savings into their future budgets, as the improvement has become "the way we do business." In other words, it's time to seek new opportunities for improvement.

The CFO or equivalent should draft the benefit realization rules and present them to the leadership team for review and ratification on or before the leader's initial Champion training. Afterwards, these rules should be communicated to all project and study Champions and practitioners. This can best be accomplished at subsequent Champion and practitioner sessions, including Green and Black Belt training. The rules should also be conveyed at team start-up training or like events when the team is first assembled. It is essential that the rules be applied consistently as each team works through their assigned project and as future teams and studies are commissioned.

Any calculated financial savings from a project must be aligned with existing business financial measures. To do otherwise will give the disastrous impression that Process Excellence employs the use of "funny money." Hard savings that contribute to EBITDA (Earnings Before Interest, Taxes, Depreciation and Amortization), also referred to as direct savings, generally have identifiable and quantifiable reductions in one or more of the following cost categories:

- Direct product material costs.
- Direct manufacturing factory costs.
- Factory overhead costs.
- Product engineering overhead costs.
- Sales, general, administrative overhead costs.
- Inventory costs.

Specific examples of direct savings include:

- Material purchase price reduction.
- Scrap reduction or improved yield at standard direct material and direct factory costs.
- Reduced labor costs resulting in specified headcount reduction of either permanent or temporary staffing.
- Reduced labor costs resulting in lower overtime premiums.
- Operating expense reductions including repair, maintenance, outside services and consumable supplies.
- Reduced utility and waste disposal costs.

- Inventory reductions at direct material and direct factory standard cost.

A project involving indirect savings may warrant additional scrutiny before permitting it to proceed. As indirect savings are generally not quantifiable, qualitative explanations of the benefit to the organization may be required. Examples of indirect savings are cost avoidance, customer and employee satisfaction, increased employee quality of life, and increased capacity with no identified growth opportunities or cost reduction.

Studies are the exception to the need for direct savings. Studies, as mentioned earlier, generally relate to research, development and engineering and involve more rapid problem-solving activities that map directly to critical knowledge gain. While often difficult to quantify in terms of cost savings, these knowledge-gaining activities are extremely important because they improve decision-making and can lead to important avenues for revenue generation. While cost savings contribute directly to organizational betterment, revenue generation is the lifeblood of an organization's future. One thing is certain: any successful Process Excellence endeavor will include revenue growth as well as cost reduction.

One final comment is appropriate regarding indirect or soft savings from DMAIC-based projects and kaizens. As your Process Excellence deployment matures, the drive for strictly hard savings benefits can be gradually relaxed. There are many worthy opportunities for improvement that will deliver soft benefits such as improvements in employee health and morale or enhanced customer satisfaction scores, which are known to lead to customer loyalty. These merit commissioning at some point, but not early on when the focus should be on quantifiable benefits that contribute to the bottom line of the business. It is always easier to migrate from hard benefits to a mixture of hard and soft benefits than to migrate from soft benefits to a combination of hard and soft benefits. So define your rules early, stick to them, and use them as a basis for screening those projects that will be commissioned from those that will not.

Best Practice

Publicize and use savings wisely.

The credibility of projects and the overall Process Excellence effort as well as wise use of Process Excellence deployment savings can be enhanced if projects are launched with a management-assigned representative from finance to assist the project team. The representative should be assigned early in a project's life cycle and should support the project team through the tasks of quantifying and verifying the project savings. As it can take time to understand and apply the leadership-approved rules for benefit calculation, determining the financial benefits can be somewhat challenging during the first wave of projects. As more teams complete projects, the process for estimating financial benefits will become more familiar, faster, and more accurate.

Savings that are generated from Process Excellence projects should benefit the business bottom line. One of our clients had a very systematic way of generating the savings and then incorporating them into the operating budget. At the start of each year the CEO would determine, based on operational requirements and financial measurements, the number of "quality dollars" that each core process/function would be required to generate. Each function would review its assigned "quality dollars" against the change that would be required in the measures of performance to achieve the desired level of benefit. Based on the cost of poor quality, measurements such as warranty costs, defect rates, scrap rates, cycle times, percent unscheduled maintenance, etc., were used to equate level of improvement to bottom line dollars. By driving tactical measures at the process level, measures at the value stream level as well as business top level indicators were impacted.

Cost centers must understand that the savings achieved by the process improvement efforts of the Process Excellence deployment are removed from subsequent years' budgets. A large and well-respected international organization having over 135 operational sites worldwide rolled out Process Excellence. Their CFO verified and removed the financial savings from all cost centers that were impacted by the commissioned project teams. When some cost centers tried to re-insert those savings into their next year's budget, the CFO intervened and disallowed the budget adjustment. Instead, the organization aggregated the savings from all projects into what was referred to as the "Bank of Operational Excellence." Each subordinate organization was given an annual savings goal. As each year progressed, each organization's actual savings were compared against their savings goals. At the end of year one, over $175M in hard savings was achieved with much of that earmarked for R&D – the lifeline of that organization. In other words, the cost savings resulting from Process Excellence were used to fund the organization's revenue growth initiative.

A properly executed Process Excellence deployment should have a documented process flow in place to show how the financial savings from each project are captured. After the savings are realized, there should be no misunderstanding. Leadership, management, and practitioners should know what happens to the money that is generated by process improvement. Everyone in the organization should be aware that a key purpose of the Process Excellence deployment is to enhance the financial bottom line of the business and that the savings from successful projects accomplish that goal. For governmental agencies and non-profit organizations, profit is not a motivator, but savings are. Thus, the comments above still apply to them as well, namely, what happens to the savings must be clearly defined. A good example of this occurred when Francis Harvey, then Secretary of the Army in 2005, deployed Lean Six Sigma throughout the entire Department of the Army. It was always perfectly clear that the savings generated by the institutional Army were to be used by the operational Army to acquire more equipment that would directly benefit the end user, the warfighter. No organization wants to exempt itself from generating improvements that result in savings that, in turn, generate further improvements. It becomes the cycle of life – and success, for which Process Excellence is the driver.

Best Practice

Regularly review projects and act based on the assessment.

As already recommended in other Best Practices, the manager should be involved in project prioritization, project selection, project progression, and successful project completion. Data from our clients demonstrates time and again that those projects having management oversight and involvement are more apt to be successful. If the manager is not involved throughout, ensuring that each phase is thoroughly interrogated/reviewed by a "hands-on," results will not be optimum.

At project review sessions, the Champion/manager of a Process Excellence project should be prepared to answer the types of questions that a CEO might raise – what is the potential impact on the operation; what is needed from the business to successfully complete the project; what strategic impact will the project have on the top level indicators; what impact will the project have on other processes, etc. To satisfy the CEO's need for business impact information, we recommend that managers brief projects and Black Belts be present to answer questions on tool usage and results achieved. Using this approach emphasizes that the business is serious about the Process Excellence deployment and the anticipated benefits.

We believe that timely project reporting at regular business reviews versus meetings devoted only to Process Excellence promotes greater management visibility and accountability. That is, project reviews should be kept as "operational" as possible. If a review process is seen as a "quality add-on," it doesn't carry the same weight as an operational review. The goal is to "operationalize" Process Excellence so it becomes part of "how we do business." When the manager is engaged in the review and is part of solving the problem, the practitioner and other team members realize that the project is important to the business. The project is seen as even weightier if it warrants getting on the schedule at business reviews. Using a combination of regularly scheduled management reviews and business reviews propels projects across the finish line more rapidly as roadblocks to the project are addressed quickly and at the appropriate level.

Businesses can use templates to help promote efficiency and effectiveness of a review. Templates should be designed with the goal of quickly presenting the current status of the project, potential roadblocks, what needs to be accomplished in the current phase of the project, a current evaluation of the ability to achieve the goals, and what help is needed from the management and leadership teams. Use of "stop light" charts is helpful in portraying project status using the following convention:

- On schedule with all DMAIC milestones: GREEN
- Behind one DMAIC milestone: YELLOW
- Behind more than one DMAIC milestone: RED

If the project is GREEN, the momentum needs to be maintained. If the project is designated as YELLOW, work needs to be done to get it on track. Projects that are designated "RED" require prompt attention by management. This usually entails infusing more resources, revising the project scope or simplifying the project, scheduling additional mentoring by an experienced coach or Master Black Belt, or even canceling the project altogether. Leaving a project in RED status indefinitely is inconsiderate to the team. It creates further waste and erodes the impact of Process Excellence on the organization. When acting on projects designated as RED, involve both the Champion who is overseeing the project and the practitioner. Remember, it is the project management Champion who is responsible and accountable for moving the project along and for providing substantive reports to management that are more than just a "dog and pony show."

There are other tools that can help leaders and managers act based on project assessments. One such tool is the Oregon Productivity Matrix (OPM) that simplifies the prioritization and resource allocation process. Raytheon has been very successful in using the OPM as a tool for identifying critical metrics relevant to the strategic decision-making process.

Best Practice

Conduct refresher sessions for leaders and practitioners.

The pace of business can sometimes be overwhelming, causing leadership and management to turn their attentions to the most pressing needs and thus making it difficult to stay focused on the strategic objectives of the organization. Even in companies where Process Excellence has been deployed to improve products and services and maintain a competitive position in the global market, there are always urgent situations that occupy the time of leaders and managers. This hectic pace with continuously surfacing urgencies may contribute to lost momentum of a Process Excellence program. In fact, the current protracted economic downturn has resulted in the postponement or outright cancellation of Process Excellence in some organizations. But research clearly indicates that process improvement efforts which incorporate the best practices highlighted in this book are precisely what must be preserved in order to survive and prosper (Source: *"An Historical Data Analysis of Business Strategies During Recessionary Times,"* by Dr. M. Kiemele, April 2010 Quality Insider online newsletter).

With all the challenges faced by leadership and managers, it should come as no surprise that the knowledge level of those who have been through an initial Process Excellence training will diminish over time.

Leaders and managers can benefit greatly by attending a short refresher session at which roles and responsibilities may be reviewed and lessons learned during the deployment can be brought up and discussed. During these sessions, leaders and managers can assess the progress to date to determine if the deployment is staying on track. Sometimes, managers trained long before they were responsible for sponsoring a project may need to be reminded to mentor the practitioner and stay engaged in all phases of the project. A review of the requirements for the tollgates and the questions that should be answered in each phase of DMAIC/IDOV may also be beneficial. Even though leaders and managers are pressed for time, the benefit of attending a refresher far exceeds the time taken to do so.

Likewise, attending refresher sessions can motivate practitioners and accelerate the progress on their projects. During a practitioner refresher session the methodology requirements and tools application should be reviewed. Lessons learned and problem-solving successes should also be discussed. A review session also provides the opportunity for networking and the exchange of ideas between people who have been involved in the early projects. The session gives the practitioner time to think about what has worked and what has not. After attending a refresher session, practitioners normally perform at a higher skill level.

The Process Excellence deployment is enhanced greatly by re-invigorating the leadership and management teams. In addition to refresher sessions, sharing ideas through the use of forums with other non-competing pioneers in change and innovation (individuals as well as companies) can be of benefit. Motivational presentations by other business leaders represent another option. Finding ways to stimulate the creativity of leadership, management, and practitioners is a continuous process that can re-vitalize and re-invigorate a Process Excellence deployment. Even though a Process Excellence initiative may be perceived as going well, leadership needs to be reminded and also remind others that good is no longer good enough. As Jim Collins says in his text *Good to Great*, "good is the enemy of great."

Best Practice

Connect and use Champions to upgrade the initiative.

A Process Excellence Champion is a strong adovcate of the initiative whose behavior is unquestionably and visibly supportive. In the early stages of a Process Excellence deployment, Champions are trained in the methodology, an overview of the tools, project selection and scoping, and their roles and responsibilities. Some Champions, also called project sponsors, quickly find themselves responsible for projects, reviewing and keeping them on track, and mentoring the practitioners. These Champions lead their projects to successful conclusion by accomplishing regular reviews and tollgating the projects at each phase of the methodology (DMAIC or IDOV), providing the necessary resources, and helping the practitioners solve issues as they arise.

Unfortunately, not all Champions become project sponsors immediately after their training. This may be because of a lack of prepared practitioners or because the Champion's processes have not yet been selected for improvement as a function of strategic prioritization. In either case, inactivity may prevent the Champion from exercising the roles and responsibilities addressed in the training session, and as time passes, the skill set may diminish. Consequently, a Champion for a project launched later in the deployment may find it hard to get a good start or maintain initial momentum. If project stagnation becomes an issue, engaging a Champion who has successfully concluded a project or identifying an experienced Champion who can assist an inexperienced Champion may help to get the project on track and keep it on track.

Champions can serve as sources of knowledge as well as sources of motivation not only for other Champions in need of help but for the overall deployment. A cadre of well seasoned Champions who have achieved Process Excellence success on projects and in deploying process improvement in their functional and departmental areas can help motivate by engaging other Champions one-on-one or in the setting of process improvement teams. Some businesses have leveraged their experienced Champion cadre by having them present success stories and lessons learned at business reviews and town hall meetings. Having Champions facilitate discussions, question and answer sessions, refresher sessions, project reviews, and deployment building events can help invigorate the initiative and generate enthusiastic and committed practitioners. Sometimes all it takes to help jump start another Champion, a process improvement effort, or the deployment in general is to hear about the successes that have been achieved. Networking and exchanging ideas can go a long way in letting others know that Process Excellence is a business effort as well as an individual effort.

Every Process Excellence practitioner needs and should seek business mentoring from a Champion as well as coaching on the proper use of the tools and methodology from a Master Black Belt or equivalent. The Champion and Master Black Belt function as a duo that must be in sync if the project is to be successfully completed in a timely manner. In mature Six Sigma organizations, Master Black Belts and Champions interrelate and work together in upgrading the initiative. In fact, in some organizations like Raytheon, Champions are expected to expand their technical competence to become certified Black Belts or Master Black Belts so that the same individual can satisfy both roles. We have long advocated that Champions ultimately become Black Belts or Master Black Belts, because it will significantly enhance the intiative. Successful Champions are valuable resources. Train them, nurture them, and use them!

Best Practice

Make everyone aware of what is going on.

For a business to be successful, it is essential that strategic objectives and deployment efforts be administered throughout the organization from top to bottom. Quality Management Systems such as the Baldrige Criteria assess the ability of an organization to achieve alignment from leadership through senior and mid-level management down to the process workers. It is harmful to an organization when administration breaks down at any level and the strategic objective is not understood, totally embraced, and properly acted upon. As a Process Excellence deployment is strategic in nature, it makes sense that it be viewed in the same light as any other strategic effort. For a Process Excellence deployment to be understood by all levels of personnel, to be properly embraced, and to be properly acted upon, everyone at every level needs to have continuing updates on the status of the deployment; and they need to know what their role in it is.

Not only is it important to have communication/information flowing vertically in the organization, it is vital that it flow horizontally along the value stream. When Process Excellence is deployed and processes are being improved, the processes along the value stream need to know what changes are taking place upstream as well as downstream. If information is not flowing, it is possible that an improvement in one process might actually result in suboptimization in the overall value stream.

One recent client was involved in worldwide shipping of trucks capable of hauling huge amounts of cargo. Because the cost involved in shipping these large trucks from one continent to another was extremely high, the business determined it was necessary to have a process improvement effort directed at reducing the costs. The shipping costs were directly related to cubic feet of the trucks being shipped. To cut down on the cubic feet of each truck being shipped, the project improvement team decided to reconfigure the trucks. Cargo bays, mirrors, holding tanks, tires, etc., were removed from the trucks and stored inside the trucks' compartments so that the surface area and cubic footage were reduced. The new process saved approximately 20% on each truck shipped, and success was declared. Three months later the business realized that the net savings were actually zero. The project team that revised the process learned from those receiving the trucks at their destination that the costs associated with reconfiguring the trucks were as much as the savings achieved by the process improvement effort. In fact, the "improved process" actually lost money when the increased use of the *process improvement resources* was taken into account. Had the truck cargo receiving team been made aware of what was going on in the process improvement effort, the cost of reconfiguring could have surfaced before the project improvement effort got too far along.

When everyone is aware of what is going on with respect to process improvement and the deployment people are engaged at all levels, the organization is aligned and the value stream process improvement efforts are enhanced. A vehicle commonly used to expand awareness is a Process Excellence awareness workshop, which some organizations refer to as White Belt training. Awareness workshops are short – typically 4-8 hour sessions that expose everyone not engaged in some other Process Excellence training venue to the need, vision, and plan for Process Excellence. Shared vocabulary and excitement are desired outputs such that participants in these workshops will want to become involved and contribute. Awareness workshops are a motivational pull system that shows participants that Process Excellence is not a closed club, but rather an open invitation for everyone to get involved in process improvement. Improvement must be in everyone's vocabulary and toolkit if Process Excellence is going to impact changing the way an organizational culture looks at and performs work.

Best Practice

Design and use standardized templates.

One of the most basic tenets of Process Excellence is variance reduction for the betterment of an organization's products, services, and processes. Why not strive to also reduce variation in the manner in which Process Excellence is deployed? Many years ago, one of our clients, EMC's Data General Division, pioneered the use of standardized Process Excellence templates. Rich Boucher, Scott Pfeffer, and Roy Potvin introduced the use of standardized templates in the area of training, project initiation, and project chartering. In time, the template library expanded to include milestone tracking, phase tollgating, project presentations, and final project report-outs. Today, the use of standardized, reusable templates is standard for those businesses seeking best practices. Templates make it easier for your Champions and practitioners to understand the tasks involved and implement each task in a more consistent manner. They also facilitate consistent communication throughout an organization.

The following tasks are recurring and merit the formulation of reusable templates for your organization:

- Project and study prioritization and selection.
- Project and study contracts or charters.
- Project and study mentoring logs.
- Project and study status reporting.

- Phase gate (e.g., DMAIC and IDOV) reviews.
- Final project and study report-outs.
- Financial benefits process checklist.
- Certification checklists.
- Certificates of completion for projects and training.
- Certification recognition.
- Knowledge Notebook for processes on which projects and studies have been completed.

Incorporate the use of your organization's existing standard templates and devise new ones as your knowledge base expands. Doing so will further help in advancing the understanding and use of Process Excellence principles, problem-solving methods, and tools.

Best Practice

Anticipate and manage position loss resulting from projects.

Most businesses embark upon Process Excellence in order to provide their customers better products and services at a cost that will allow the business to make a profit. As a result of improvement, processes are often able to perform with less manpower, allowing for a reduction in staffing requirements. In such cases, businesses are frequently willing to move the resulting surplus resources to other functions and let normal attrition take care of the excess manpower.

Many leaders *assure* their workforce that headcount reductions will be absorbed through attrition and that there should be no job loss as a result of a Process Excellence improvement initiative. Even with this assurance from leaders and managers, the workforce will scrutinize the deployment impact on headcount. Any perception of making a process so "excellent" that it removes the improver's own job will be detrimental to a Process Excellence endeavor. One way to avoid the concern that employees will view manpower reductions as a result of Process Excellence is for the business to reduce to the desired/required staffing level as a function of a business financial decision. After the reduction is made, the Process Excellence deployment can serve as the vehicle to help workers develop the skills to perform the processes and services even better than before the reduction.

If all or part of your organization's workforce is unionized, representatives from union leadership should be involved from the start of the Process Excellence deployment. Many of our clients have found it helpful to include the union leadership in the initial training of business leaders and managers. Knowing the principles of Process Excellence and the need, vision, and plan, the union leadership can help articulate to the process workers the importance of the deployment and can help reduce the concerns and fears that the workers may express. Union leadership support is more likely to be offered if it is convinced that the deployment is not bringing about the reduction in headcount.

The message from leadership should be that any reduction in labor costs/headcount is a function of business reality and not directly linked to Process Excellence. The sponsoring CEO/President should make this clear early on as part of the stated need, vision, and plan for the organization's Process Excellence deployment.

Best Practice

Include team-oriented "soft" tools.

Newly trained Process Excellence practitioners are generally quite excited about applying their tools knowledge to the projects they have been assigned by their management. It is generally accepted by Champions and practitioners that tools are vital to process improvement. What is sometimes not as well understood is that the soft skills can be equally important, because trying to change someone's personality and mindset is extremely difficult if not impossible. Without the soft skills required to lead team endeavors, practitioners may find that successful conclusions to projects are elusive. The following are some soft skills that an effective Champion or practitioner should possess:

- Inspires others to excel.
- Challenges others to be creative.
- Leads change by challenging conventional wisdom, developing and applying new methodologies, and creating innovative strategies.
- Is creative and a critical, out-of-the box thinker.
- Allows room for failures and mistakes with plan to recover.
- Accepts responsibility for choices.
- Responds well to criticism.
- Encourages commitment, dedication and teamwork.
- Unites a team to a core purpose.
- Communicates all sides of an issue.
- Solicits diverse ideas and viewpoints.
- Shows empathy.
- Works on win-win solutions.

While it is difficult to find someone who could score a "perfect 10" in each of these areas, there are "soft" tools that can be learned and applied. Since a project team's success is closely linked to the success of its meetings, "soft" tools for making team decisions, such as multi-voting, brainstorming, nominal group technique, and pairwise comparison, should be addressed in the training received by Champions and practitioners. Those leading teams must know how to complete a stakeholder analysis, develop and implement a communications plan, and utilize the skill set of each team member while maintaining focus on successful project completion. Knowing and applying Kotter's Change Model, as well as understanding and appreciating the "WIIFM" (What's In It For Me) concept, will undoubtedly increase the effectiveness of any Process Excellence Champion or practitioner.

The best process improvement efforts are achieved by teams that can blend the knowledge gained through the application of the hard tools of DMAIC, IDOV, etc., with the application of the "soft" tools. This combination will help unite the team while capitalizing on the strengths of the individual team members. Competency in soft skills pays dividends.

Best Practice

Develop transfer functions to predict, optimize, and assess risk.

At a recent Lean Six Sigma (LSS) conference, a LSS Deployment Leader at a well-known company related that they don't use Design of Experiments (DOE) because they are a transactional company and don't need to use it. What he was saying is heresy to the authors.

What we "heard" him say was, "we don't need to predict, optimize, or assess risk. Furthermore, we make decisions based on facts and data, but we don't need to know the best data collection techniques available today." DOE is the gateway to building transfer functions which allows practitioners at all levels and in all walks of life to predict, assess risk, determine cause and effect relationships, and to optimize their products and processes. A very simple definition of a transfer function is $y=f(x)$, namely, a relationship between inputs and outputs of any process. A validated transfer function is the most compact way of storing information and knowledge about a process. Lacking a transfer function, we are limited to changing one factor at a time (OFAT) like a doctor commonly does when changing one thing (like the dosage of a medication) and then observing if the symptoms of the problem have been mitigated.

Air Academy Associates uses as a yardstick for assessing the maturity of any Process Excellence program the metric of percentage of critical-to-customer performance measures (CTCs) for which validated transfer functions exist. Sometimes transfer functions are known. When they are not, and that is generally the case, DOE is the mechanism for developing and validating them. In essence, DOE is the science of data collection because it provides the most effective and efficient way to collect data when trying to establish relationships and test for cause and effect. Without it, we cannot even begin to develop the transfer functions needed to be competitive in the market place. It is amazing how many performance improvement experts dabble for decades in the noise cloud without ever once trying to escape it and extend their process and product knowledge quickly and at low cost. Google has escaped the noise cloud and is one company that relies heavily on DOE. When we make a query using Google, we want answers quickly. Google thinks of a query as an opportunity to experiment and does so very wisely, using DOE to maximize the value of a "click."

Transfer functions apply across all areas, including marketing, human resources, healthcare, financial institutions, etc. Conjoint analysis is a term given to the application of DOE in marketing in order to develop critical relationships between a response variable (y) and various predictor variables (x's). Bank of America develops transfer functions to determine the critical factors associated with human resource turnover rates. In healthcare, transfer functions have been developed to minimize renal transplant rejection, reduce post-anesthesia nausea, and determine the most critical factors contributing to the spread of AIDS. Banking institutions develop transfer functions to generate profiles of those most likely to default on loans. Validated transfer functions enable decision makers to change "I think" to "I know."

Recalling the early days of Six Sigma at a major client of ours when the leaders of the company were attending Champion training, a major question in the training venue was always "where is the meat?" Well, the meat of Six Sigma or any Process Excellence initiative lies in the ability to predict and assess risk based on an optimized process. A major difference between good and bad leaders is the ability to predict reliably and repeatedly. If the reader has not experienced the power of transfer functions or has not acquired the ability to develop them, he or she is missing out on the "meat" of Process Excellence. It is time for leaders and managers to develop this capability in their companies and bring in the "meat" for competitive advantage.

The development of validated transfer functions is one of the Top Five Best Practices for generating step change in process and product knowledge and, consequently, return on investment. Yet it is often dismissed as something we don't need to do because it is a "manufacturing thing." The lack of transfer functions is also linked to a lack of mathematical maturity in the rank and file. We live in a culture that says mathematics is for nerds. Fortunately, with today's technology, one does not have to be a nerd to develop transfer functions. Only the desire to know what a transfer function is and how it can help is needed.

Best Practice

Make innovation systematic.

We view Process Excellence as an overarching set of principles, problem-solving methods, and tools for improving any organization's products, processes, and services. The use of Lean for improving flow and Six Sigma for reducing variation employs the Define > Measure > Analyze > Improve > Control (DMAIC) problem-solving / process-improvement methodology. Lean Six Sigma (LSS) utilizes tools having low to high levels of complexity that are capable of improving virtually any value stream – be it from design to early pilot production, order entry to order delivery, time from loan application to approved/declined, etc. Design for Six Sigma (DFSS) employs the Identify>Design>Optimize>Validate (IDOV) problem-solving methodology and focuses primarily on design and engineering value streams, such as concept to commercialization. It uses more advanced tools. We recommend that the capabilities of both LSS and DFSS be developed early on in your Process Excellence rollout. Doing so will yield benefits from their collective synergy and significantly increase your bottom line as opposed to deploying one or the other alone. It is often the case that if the improvement shown in the Improve phase of DMAIC is not sufficient, then IDOV will be invoked. Systematic innovation is needed to enhance the capability and integration of both methodologies and to deliver both top-line and bottom-line growth.

The imperative to innovate is unrelenting. Innovation means the creation of a new or radically improved product or service that is useful for some segment of society. Innovation requires a vision to see beyond where products and services are now and a means to deliver that visionary value to customers in ways the customer may not have even thought about. But what exactly is "systematic" innovation? Systematic innovation is used here to denote a structured approach to innovation that is repeatable, reliable, and predictable. It does not mean waiting for the organization's creative geniuses to come up with their next epiphany. No organization can bet its future on the creative surges of a select few. Everyone must be involved, and that is why innovation must become systematic in an organization that wants to use Process Excellence to become competitively excellent.

We highly recommend that your Process Excellence rollout include training and coaching in systematic innovation. This training will necessarily include Psychological and Emotional Methods of Creativity (PEM), Theory of Inventive Problem Solving (TRIZ), robust and tolerance design, and the use of predictive methods to assess product and/or process capability before actual production or process implementation begins. Also, soft tools are as important, if not more so, than the hard tools referenced above. See Best Practice No. 37.

Topics such as those mentioned below need to be discussed, planned for, and implemented:

- How should your innovation teams be manned, structured, managed, and held accountable?
- What is their initial vision and plan?
- How should their hand-offs and approvals facilitate their learning process and accountability?
- How will innovation teams interface with the rest of the organization and its customers?
- How can the organization's culture cultivate innovation in a sustainable way over time while continuing to face unprecedented risks and uncertainties?
- What milestones or metrics will these teams employ and how will the feedback from their customers, often referred to as early adopters, be gauged?
- How will rapid iteration in their work be assured and accelerated using the analogy of small batches to allow the teams to make mistakes quickly, facilitate learning, pivot or persevere, and start again?
- As successful innovation is demonstrated, how will these products and services be integrated into the organization's overall portfolio of products and services?
- How will the management of these innovation teams be cultivated within the organization over time to foster creativity and entrepreneurship?

Weaving both hard and soft tools within the Process Excellence umbrella will allow innovation to become a reality for a broad cross-section of your employees, not just those who reside in your research, development, or engineering organizations. While there are those who believe that Innovation and Process Excellence cannot peacefully coexist, the data says they can. In fact, Process Excellence is a nurturing environment for Innovation, according to researchers Allen and Davenport at Babson College. Their article in *Quality Progress Magazine* (September 2009) reports on a longitudinal study of 35 companies that implemented innovation. They found that the companies having a strong Process Excellence initiative in place were successful 90% of the time, whereas those that didn't were successful in implementing innovation only 35% of the time. That is a statistically significant result.

If you plan on using an external service provider for Process Excellence, it is suggested that one be selected having verifiable credentials and experience spanning all of the required elements including Lean, Six Sigma, Design for Six Sigma, PEM, TRIZ, etc. Using a single, high quality provider will also yield greater consistency, efficiency, proficiency and self-sustainability at a lower cost.

Best Practice

Solve new problems using trained resources and trumpet successes.

This best practice may seem like common sense, but common sense is not always common practice. New problems continue to crop up seemingly at random in every organization. And the solutions to these problems may take higher precedence than the solutions for problems already in the queue awaiting resolution via Process Excellence projects. Have you ever been in a situation where an officer of the company was presented with a burning issue and immediately prescribed one or more solutions, along with who would be in charge of their implementation? Such "go change this – we can't wait" events occur frequently. When they do, consideration must be given to using your organization's Process Excellence resources to help. It is precisely for such burning issues that Process Excellence is designed. Yet at times leaders and managers don't recognize that Process Excellence Champions and practitioners are trained to address these very issues. It's as if some leaders and managers believe that Process Excellence is reserved for a certain category of problems.

A common pitfall in problem resolution is prescribing a solution in advance. This is where Process Excellence expertise can really help. Process Excellence practitioners are trained to let the data, tools, and teams – not opinions – drive the solutions through root cause discovery. If opinion drives the change or solution, chances are you will be addressing this issue again and probably soon. Foster the use of your Process Excellence investments – the people, principles, methods, and tools – to help solve any tactical or strategic problem. At first, Process Excellence resources may require the support of coaches, so leaders and managers should be patient. But as the practitioners become more experienced, Process Excellence can and should be used to solve an organization's toughest problems. Don't cut Process Excellence short. Demand the most from it, and use it! Or you will lose it.

Since success itself is the best predictor of success, it is important to trumpet significant results. Whether we think so or not, Process Excellence needs to be sold inside the organization. What better way than to show that it works, and that it works on significant issues? This also gives leadership the chance to recognize the Champions and practitioners who have delivered the success stories.

Best Practice

Make Process Excellence part of the human resource succession plan.

Recognize those practitioners who reliably, repeatedly, and predictably lead and complete Process Excellence projects and studies that yield impactful results. One key way to accomplish this is to promote such individuals. They should also be included in your organization's succession plan. The percentage of individuals who are on the succession plan list and who are top-tier certified Process Excellence practitioners should increase over time. Increasing the opportunities for advancement provides added incentive to serve in a Process Excellence capacity.

In essence, if we want to develop a Process Excellence culture, then we need to link promotion to Process Excellence. Selecting the right people up front for key Process Excellence positions (Champions and practitioners) will naturally propagate the leadership pipeline. But there are always those late bloomers who should not be dismissed. Their involvement in Process Excellence makes it possible to discover them.

Best Practice

Integrate Process Excellence into all mergers and acquisitions.

The number of mergers and acquisitions varies over time, often as a function of the economy. Historical data strongly support the fact that investments in Process Excellence, including the implementation of systematic innovation, must be sustained – not reduced or eliminated – when mergers and acquisitions occur. To the greatest extent possible, the CEOs and Champions involved in these events need to preserve the momentum and achievements realized from Process Excellence. This is no trivial task.

Merging two disparate organizations, each having its own culture and programs for improvement, requires a detailed analysis. The importance of aligning the common Process Excellence terms and language post-merger/acquisition cannot be overstated. Even though developing a common Process Excellence language is a daunting task, it is one of the most critical activities within the merger and acquisition process. Process Excellence and its related activities must be a major part of the due diligence process in acquiring another organization. The merged effort must capitalize on the strengths from each organization while reducing or eliminating any weaknesses. The new organization's Process Excellence effort should, therefore, be more capable in benefit delivery than the sum of the affected organizations' earlier efforts in change.

When the authors think of mergers and acquisitions, a premier company that comes to mind with regard to Process Excellence is Danaher Corporation. Danaher is comprised of dozens of different businesses. Despite its many mergers and acquisitions, it has stayed true to its commitment to Process Excellence by using its Danaher Business System to align all of its businesses under a common Process Excellence framework. The result has been a positive impact on all of the Danaher businesses.

Best Practice

 Update the implementation plan based on feedback and results.

Implementation plans should be routinely assessed to determine if the intended results are being achieved. The best plans take into account today's economic uncertainty and what that means for the organization. It is wasteful and contrary to the purpose of Process Excellence to implement a plan and not make mid-course corrections despite feedback that indicates change is warranted.

The 12-18 month Process Excellence implementation plan should be evaluated to understand and reduce the gap between the estimated benefits and the actual benefits that accrue over time. We suggest that performance-to-plan assessments be accomplished at least semi-annually. The following areas of performance are recommended for review as part of these assessments:

- Leadership alignment and support.
- Project/study/Rapid Improvement Event (RIE) selection.
- Project/study/RIE execution.
- Benefit capture.
- Knowledge gain and sharing.
- Deployment planning.
- Champion and practitioner performance.
- Degree of self-sustainability (see Best Practices No. 8 and No. 21).
- Results (actual versus expected).
- Culture change.

Regarding the last bullet, culture change, it may take years to see a significant shift in this area. The interested reader is referred to George Eckes' excellent book: *Making Six Sigma Last: Managing the Balance Between Cultural and Technical Change.*

The assessments should be fact versus opinion-based to the maximum extent possible. Data must support any statements obtained through interviews. Assessments should involve all major business units and the corporate headquarters. Though often not included, headquarters processes that affect the entire organization are ripe for improvement and merit the commissioning of Process Excellence projects led by Champions and practitioners residing on the headquarters staff. Oftentimes, project results and recommendations coming out of headquarters conflict with project results from the business units. Assessments can help resolve such issues.

Once all of the assessment data has been gathered and summarized, it should be presented to the organization's full leadership, including the corporate staff, for review and action. We recommend reviewing assessment data for a given business unit with that unit's operating President before the corporate-wide data is presented to the full leadership team. Following this review, the deployment plan should be revised to incorporate changes as appropriate.

Financial and Implementation Accountability		
No.	Best Practice	Self-Assess Your Degree of Implementation (0-Min, 2-Max)
19.	Use a consistent, simple and straightforward approach.	
20.	Generate successes early and communicate them.	
21.	Plan the service provider's exit strategy.	
22.	Develop internal subject matter experts.	
23.	Manage the expectations of every practitioner.	
24.	Define and use a meaty certification process.	
25.	Train all areas of the organization.	
26.	Apply the training immediately.	
27.	Provide expert coaching on all projects and studies.	
28.	Scope projects carefully.	
29.	Establish and follow rules for assessing benefits.	
30.	Publicize and use savings wisely.	
31.	Regularly review projects and act based on the assessment.	
32.	Conduct refresher sessions for leaders and practitioners.	
33.	Connect and use Champions to upgrade the initiative.	
34.	Make everyone aware of what is going on.	
35.	Design and use standardized templates.	
36.	Anticipate and manage position loss resulting from projects.	
37.	Include team-oriented "soft" tools.	

Financial and Implementation Accountability		
No.	Best Practice	Self-Assess Your Degree of Implementation (0-Min, 2-Max)
38.	Develop transfer functions to predict, optimize, and assess risk.	
39.	Make innovation systematic.	
40.	Solve new problems using trained resources and trumpet successes.	
41.	Make Process Excellence part of the human resource succession plan.	
42.	Integrate Process Excellence into all mergers and acquisitions.	
43.	Update the implementation plan based on feedback and results.	
	Total (Max = 50):	

Table 6:
Checklist Summary for Chapter 6

Chapter 7

Reward and Recognition

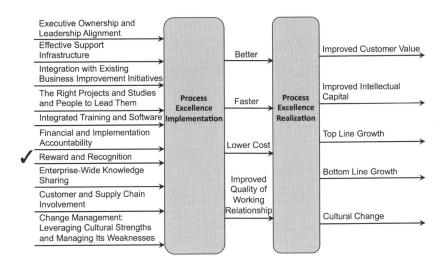

"Doing the best at this moment puts you in the best place for the next moment."

Oprah Winfrey
American Media Proprietor, Talk Show Host, Actress, Producer and
Philanthropist

Best Practice

Recognize people who execute successful projects.

Earnest work merits timely recognition. Those involved on project and study teams that solve real problems and yield verifiable benefits deserve recognition. The intent for such recognition is not only to praise such efforts, but to also drive the right behavior. There is no better way to propagate the cultural influence of Process Excellence than to show that it works and to recognize those involved. People should want to be part of Process Excellence and not be forced into it. In general, non-monetary forms of recognition are recommended. One of our clients surveyed their practitioners to help understand preferences and tailor recognition to the individual (e.g., dinner certificates, recognition in company publications, etc.). We have had clients that offered team members a percentage of the independently verifiable savings attained by that project team. There are problems with this arrangement, including employee motivation to serve exclusively on projects showing the potential for large savings. Peer recognition is a powerful motivator and should be used whenever possible in the context of Process Excellence.

Monetary incentives may become a key motivator for executing projects *after* a Process Excellence practitioner is certified. To imbed Process Excellence in the culture, it will take more than doing just the projects that lead to certification. It is what comes after certification that determines if Process Excellence is sticking. The "one and done" syndrome is alive and well in many companies. That is, a practitioner accomplishes enough project work (perhaps only one) to become certified. Then what? Has that person accomplished any successful projects after certification? A metric we are now using to help assess the cultural impact of Process Excellence is the number of successful (true problem solving with verifiable benefit to the organization) post-certification projects being accomplished. As the number of certified Agents grows, this number should also grow. The jury is still out regarding monetary incentives for post-certification projects. Long-term studies are needed to determine the effect. Ideally, a designed experiment should be conducted, but it will be a long one and organizations hesitate to participate in such a long-term study, especially in this economy.

In the context of Process Excellence, a blend of formal and informal recognition is recommended. The following examples illustrate some options:

Formal Avenues of Recognition

- Deferred stock options.
- One-time cash bonuses.
- Merit increases in pay.
- Awarding certification.

Informal Avenues of Recognition

- All-hands employee reviews.

- Newsletters.
- Shareholder meetings.
- Customer/supplier forums.
- Selection of a gift as part of an existing corporate recognition program.
- "Night on the town" including a meal and show for employee and spouse.
- Inscription of certification status on employee business cards.

As Eric Ries mentioned in his text entitled *The Lean Startup,* even having one's name on the door can serve as a highly meaningful form of recognition.

Remember, all project and study efforts that successfully complete a management-approved task in accordance with their original mandate deserve recognition, even if the benefit to the business is added knowledge alone.

Reward & Recognition		
No.	Best Practice	Self-Assess Your Degree of Implementation (0-Min, 2-Max)
44.	Recognize people who execute successful projects.	
Total (Max = 2):		

Table 7:
Checklist Summary for Chapter 7

Chapter 8

Enterprise-Wide Knowledge Sharing

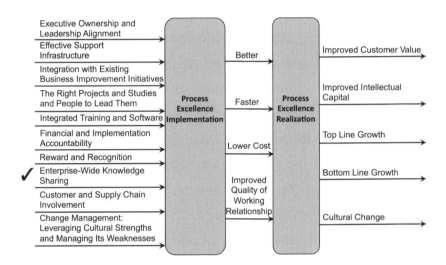

"It ain't what you don't know that gets you; it's the things you know that ain't so."

Mark Twain
American Author and Humorist

Best Practice

Establish a project-tracking database and keep it current.

Project and study tracking is facilitated by using enterprise-wide software. Possessing this capability assists management by tracking the strategic alignment of the projects and studies being commissioned. It also aids in assessing how each project is progressing over time with regard to gate reviews and in measuring the nature (e.g., hard versus soft) and actual amount of benefits accumulated over time. Project-tracking software allows us to keep track of our return on investment (ROI) from Process Excellence. After all, Process Excellence is an investment.

Enterprise-wide software can also track programmatic issues of importance relative to Process Excellence, including certification levels, upcoming training events, promotion and retention of certified practitioners, etc. Enterprise-wide project and study tracking software can also aid in the actual selection and prioritization of projects and studies. It can signal potential problems such as excessive average cycle times for projects and large gaps between actual and expected benefits. It is also a vehicle to share information and communicate project results as well as key lessons learned. Being able to track key implementation metrics promotes greater accountability, particularly for management to become more involved in the projects and studies for which they have oversight and responsibility.

Select your Process Excellence metrics wisely. Measuring the number of teams, amount of money saved, and number of employees certified may represent little more than vanity metrics that portray an optimistic picture. Alternatively, measuring Belt retention over time, the number of post certification projects, average project/study savings after multiple cycles of learning, and the ability to attract greater cross sections of the workforce as Process Excellence gains greater traction over time, etc., can serve as better examples of more actionable and meaningful metrics.

We definitely encourage the use of project-tracking software. However, its development, implementation, and refinement can become a distraction, especially during the all-important first year of deploying Process Excellence. The following suggestions are offered:

- Though development can proceed in year one of the rollout, delay implementation until after proof-of-concept has occurred.
- Use Microsoft® Excel® spreadsheets to the extent possible during year one and keep it simple.
- Use internal software systems and human resources to the greatest extent possible.
- Detail your requirements upfront and ensure that subsequent changes can be readily accomplished. That is, use DFSS principles to develop this project tracking software.
- Ensure simplicity of use by those involved in project and study management and execution.

- The system, as well as the effort put into this product, should be aligned with the magnitude of the rollout.
- Use this capability at regular management reviews.
- Weave training on how to use this capability into Process Excellence-related training.
- Assess the usefulness of this capability over time as part of assessing the overall effectiveness of Process Excellence.

Whether your organization opts to invest in an enterprise-wide project and study tracking system or to use simple spreadsheets (at least at the outset of the deployment), the CEO/President along with his or her staff will need a simple, effective, and fact-based capability of knowing where Process Excellence stands at any point in time.

Best Practice

Schedule benchmarking sessions.

As our colleague, George Maszle, aptly and recently said, "We get so trapped in our improvement process thinking that it is difficult to look at things differently." Process Excellence efforts need to be re-vitalized over time. Do not rely solely on the good counsel and suggestions of your service provider or what you read online or in print concerning like programs at other organizations. Your organization will need to benchmark with other trendsetters in improvement and innovation on a *regular* basis. That means benchmarking is not only for those who are starting out but also for those who have well-established Process Excellence programs. Remember Jim Collins' famous quote: "good is the enemy of great." When benchmarking, compare not only metrics but also process as well. The 50 Best Practices in this book would be a good standard on which to compare with others. Benchmarking must be one of the key tasks contained within your Process Excellence deployment plan.

Be selective in the organizations you decide to benchmark with and equally selective in any conferences you opt to attend for benchmarking. If you return from a given conference with less than three substantial ideas for re-vitalizing key aspects of your ongoing investment in Process Excellence, your attendance at that conference fell into your organization's Cost of Waste bucket. Keep in mind, also, that presentations at conferences do not always convey the true state of nature at a particular company.

Reciprocate with those with whom you benchmark. Invite CEOs and Presidents from other organizations to meet with your CEO and President and his or her staff. They, too, need and deserve regular doses of inspiration to be effective in planning, operating, and improving all aspects of the organization. Make benchmarking a win-win opportunity.

Enterprise-Wide Knowledge Sharing		
No.	Best Practice	Self-Assess Your Degree of Implementation (0-Min, 2-Max)
45.	Establish a project-tracking database and keep it current.	
46.	Schedule benchmarking sessions.	
	Total (Max = 4):	

Table 8:
Checklist Summary for Chapter 8

Chapter 9

Customer and Supply Chain Involvement

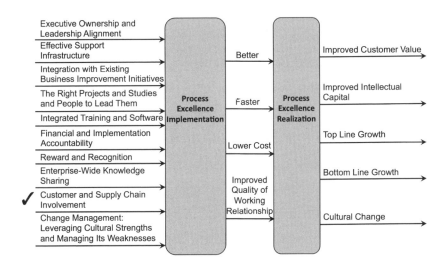

"Coming together is a beginning. Keeping together is progress. Working together is success."

Henry Ford
American Industrialist, Founder of the Ford Motor Company and Sponsor
of the Development of the Assembly Line Technique of Mass Production

Best Practice

Involve suppliers and customers early on.

Include your key customers and suppliers in solving problems of joint concern using the principles, methodologies, and tools associated with Process Excellence. Doing so will benefit the entire value chain and simultaneously improve the quality of your working relationships with these important stakeholders. We encourage this practice early on but not until your organization has a handle on its own processes. Once you have your own act together, then one can look for potential joint projects. One way to begin this effort is to identify one or more specific problems faced by your organization and your customer and/or supplier. Next, assign a project Champion and Belts (or Belt candidates if this is their first formal exposure to Process Excellence) from both organizations that are knowledgeable about the problem. Have these individuals formulate a project or study contract and related Input-Process-Output diagram and enroll them in an upcoming Green or Black Belt training class. Complete the project in accordance with the project contract and include each project's status at regular internal management reviews as well as at reviews between your organization and each customer or supplier that is involved in these efforts. Stakeholder analysis is critical in these joint projects, and this must be done in excruciating detail if the project is going to be a win-win effort.

A large, multi-national client commissioned its first wave of Lean Six Sigma Black Belt training and invited a key supplier involved in a long-standing problem to participate in that early wave of training. The problem related to long delays in returning repaired electronic equipment. The repair process involved diagnostics performed at the client's facilities, re-packaging, and sending the equipment to the supplier's repair depots in Mexico. The items were repaired and then sent back to one of several client facilities for resale. A Belt candidate from both the client and supplier underwent Black Belt training together at the client's facility. Their team used the DMAIC problem-solving methodology and related tools to reduce the average cycle time by 50% and also reduce the average repair cost by 35%. The client paid for the tuition associated with this training while the supplier covered all of the travel and related expenses. The relationship between this client and its supplier improved and additional projects benefitting both parties were subsequently commissioned.

Anticipate requests for price decreases from your customers as a result of savings created from joint projects. Price reduction requests should not, however, discourage you from commissioning such efforts as the benefits in terms of having a more satisfied customer and a healthier long-term relationship with that customer outweigh any near-term reductions in profit. Again, we recommend a detailed stakeholder analysis to make sure everyone knows where everyone else sits with regard to the potential results and ramifications of the project.

Implement a fact-based process for assessing the Voice of the Customer.

The means by which any organization plans, operates, and improves must necessarily involve a *systematic*, *continuous*, and *fact-based* process for understanding the Voice of the Customer (VOC). This is particularly true when designing new products, processes, and services. In this context, identifying customer requirements and looking for opportunities to solve problems for the customer that may not even be articulated are key components for understanding the VOC. You can make the best buggy whips in the world, but if nobody wants buggy whips, then sales will be low. Understanding the true VOC and translating the customer's vernacular into meaningful measures is one of the most difficult tasks in Process Excellence. A team is needed to undertake such a daunting task.

The project team should be cross-functional in nature and involve people from all stages in the life cycle of a product or service. Customer requirements need to be translated and prioritized into a set of "critical-to-customer" (CTC) functional requirements, each of which must be measurable. If they are not measurable, they cannot be improved. A commonly used tool to perform this translation and prioritization is the "first House of Quality" in quality function deployment (QFD). Obtaining and measuring the VOC is no easy task and is often an iterative process. It may involve tools like design of experiments (DOE) or conjoint analysis to discover the true VOC. In many cases, customers may not know their requirements. Furthermore, what they tell you may not be exactly what they really mean. Truth in the VOC realm is elusive, and there can be huge differences between customers with regard to their individual needs and wants. This will require patience and a high degree of collaboration between your organization and your customers. This may involve observing real customer behavior, facilitating the interaction with real customers, and behaving rationally when customers act in unexpected ways.

Many organizations deliberately limit contact between their key employee position holders and their customer counterparts. This limits the ability of the organization to learn, understand, and act on matters of importance to the customer.

A critical tool used in new product or process development is the DFSS scorecard. A DFSS scorecard comprises four major areas: parts, process, performance, and software. Using metrics such as defects per unit (dpu), both the within-area and between-area capabilities can be combined. The project manager can then easily detect where the greatest opportunities lie. The DFSS scorecard is also a powerful way to reallocate resources as necessary and is central to selecting the right projects or studies.

VOC must also impact your non-design related projects. If you commission projects that exclusively yield internal benefits without benefiting your customers in terms of product or service quality, cost, or timeliness in their delivery, then your Process Excellence efforts have been short-sighted. The only exception is when such exclusivity is justified to preserve the organization until such time as it attains a sound financial footing. However, one must always remember that the source of finances is the customer. Tools such as Pugh concept selection, pairwise comparisons, project rating matrix, and a VOC benefit /effort grid will be useful to ensure your customer's requirements are appropriately factored into the selection of future projects and studies. Please reference Air Academy Associates' text *Design for Six Sigma: The Tool Guide for Practitioners* for more detail on these and other VOC-related tools.

Customer & Supply Chain Involvement		
No.	Best Practice	Self-Assess Your Degree of Implementation (0-Min, 2-Max)
47.	Involve suppliers and customers early on.	
48.	Implement a fact-based process for assessing the Voice of the Customer.	
Total (Max = 4):		

Table 9:
Checklist Summary for Chapter 9

Chapter 10

Change Management: Leveraging Cultural Strengths and Managing Its Weaknesses

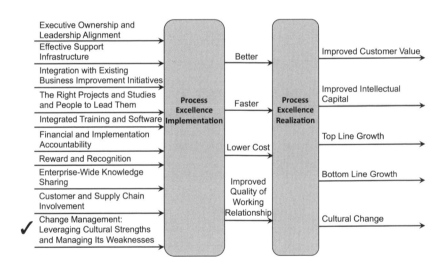

Executive Ownership and Leadership Alignment				
Effective Support Infrastructure		Better		Improved Customer Value
Integration with Existing Business Improvement Initiatives				
The Right Projects and Studies and People to Lead Them	Process Excellence Implementation	Faster	Process Excellence Realization	Improved Intellectual Capital
Integrated Training and Software				
Financial and Implementation Accountability		Lower Cost		Top Line Growth
Reward and Recognition				
Enterprise-Wide Knowledge Sharing		Improved Quality of Working Relationship		Bottom Line Growth
Customer and Supply Chain Involvement				
✓ Change Management: Leveraging Cultural Strengths and Managing Its Weaknesses				Cultural Change

"We must take change by the hand or rest assuredly, change will take us by the throat."

Winston Churchill
British Prime Minister, Statesmen, Orator, Historian, Nobel Laureate and Honorary Citizen of the United States

Best Practice

View Process Excellence as a mindset, not just a toolset.

The goal of any Process Excellence effort is for the organization to significantly increase its top and bottom lines, improve its level of customer satisfaction, enhance its intellectual capital, and anchor all of these through culture change. The words "culture" and "change" mean different things to different people, but putting them together confounds them even more. Many leaders have a vision for change and have activated that vision through a program that commissions projects and teams to drive a culture of change by executing projects in order to achieve the goals stated above. In a sense, each project is a change initiative – at the micro level – because something has to change in order to improve a process. Like my mother once told me, "Change or you'll stay that way."

But how do we get lasting and positive change at the macro level (i.e., organizationally) so that improvement and excellence become the norm? Probably, no subject has received as much attention as this one. From *Leading Change* (John Kotter) to *Who Killed Change* (Blanchard, et al), the literature is replete with "how to's" for driving organizational change. One thing is certain: there are many necessary conditions for generating organizational change. No doubt one of the necessary conditions is the way we think about improving processes. The Process Excellence mindset involves asking and answering the right questions using the appropriate tools, not using tools for the sake of using tools. Leaders and managers can begin using and internalizing the "Questions Leaders Need to Ask" that are discussed in detail in Air Academy Associates' text *Knowledge Based Management*. These questions form a "pull system" for the use of the proper tools and methods that will help improve processes and products. Leaders and managers exercising these questions on a daily basis will change the lexicon to one of using facts and data for better decision-making. And that is the ultimate necessary condition for achieving the goals stated above. Successful companies find that using the Process Excellence tools to answer questions evokes powerful conversations that aid improvement activities. As Steve LeClaire at EMC once said, "The power of the tools is in the conversations they create."

Repeatedly exercising the DMAIC (Define > Measure > Analyze > Improve > Control) and IDOV (Identify > Design > Optimize > Validate) problem-solving methodologies will help solidify the scientific method in the hearts and minds of practitioners − hopefully to the point where it becomes automatic. Unfortunately, for some it will never become automatic; but Kotter has documented that culture change can take place even though not everyone is on board. However, a committed core is necessary in order to attain the critical mass needed for culture change. This best practice, along with Best Practice No. 3 (Train the Leadership

First), constitutes one of the "top five" critical areas for a successful deployment.

A characteristic observed repeatedly over the last 30 years that indicates one has NOT internalized Process Excellence into the thought process is when one does NOT consider variation as a major deterrent to process and product excellence. Variation is the enemy in any customer-touching process, and it is a major contributor to every imaginable kind of waste. Until we try to understand variation's impact and control it, waste will continue to consume us. A common response in a recent iSixSigma survey is, "Our Six Sigma program is doomed because our new CEO does not like Six Sigma." We also hear from some that they are not supporters of Six Sigma. We like to flip this conversation by stating that Six Sigma is an Improvement Program. Are they not supporters of improvement? This line of reasoning seems to work in resetting their perspective. Not knowing the difference between label and substance is a clear indicator that Process Excellence is not part of the thought process or mindset. Another common statement, "we want Lean but don't want anything to do with Six Sigma," is an indication that the speaker has no idea of the impact that variation has on the infamous 7 or 8 wastes targeted by Lean. The jargon of CAVE (Citizens Against Virtually Everything) people is evidence that Process Excellence is not part of their thought process.

Since a major theme running throughout all of Process Excellence is measuring key performance measures and improving them, we must also attempt to measure the impact Process Excellence has on the culture of an organization. Though we have mentioned this previously in Best Practice No. 44, we feel it is so important that we reiterate it here. The number of successful "post-certification" projects or studies per certified practitioner per year seems to be a good indicator of how well Process Excellence has taken hold and has become part of the mindset of an organization.

Best Practice

Leverage cultural strengths that promote change.

As Tom Quan, Director of Engineering at Apotex, once said at a leadership review, "When culture and change compete, culture wins." Eric Ries, author of *The Lean Startup*, stated, "Process is the only foundation upon which a great company culture can develop." Though this best practice is the last of the 50 Process Excellence Best Practices, its importance cannot be overstated.

Culture represents a set of norms by which an organization functions. Norms can be further defined as an organization's set of written and unwritten policies, procedures, and processes by which it operates. There are no two cultures that are identical. Each organization has its own unique norms that set it apart from others. That is why no two rollouts of Process Excellence can be identical. In the context of Process Excellence, the challenge is to leverage those norms that support change while managing or overcoming those that are contrary to it. It is because organizations fail to meet this challenge that well over 50% of Process Excellence rollouts fall well short of their goals in the first year alone.

What is an example of a cultural norm that supports fact-based, systematic, and continuous change? One of our large multi-national clients had a long-standing policy of linking an individual's quarterly goal sheet to his/her compensation. If an important set of actions or activities had to be accomplished in a timely and quality manner, these actions or activities would be entered into an individual's quarterly goal sheet. If these were accomplished on time and with the level of quality specified, a portion of that person's total quarterly compensation would be granted to that individual. If not, full compensation might not be granted. When Process Excellence was initiated within the organization, project completion was incorporated into the quarterly goal sheets of those involved. Adding projects as goals did not ensure their timely completion, but it sure helped.

What about a cultural norm that is contrary to promoting the principles of change as espoused by Process Excellence? The same client mentioned above had a practice in place whereby major problems were corrected by sending one or more engineering/service personnel to the customer site until the problem(s) was (were) resolved. If the personnel accomplished this task in a timely and effective manner, they were rewarded financially. While quickly correcting such deficiencies for customers is paramount, especially in the purchase of expensive and complex systems and equipment, fixing the *process* to effectively prevent a problem's reoccurrence is even more important. This same organization seldom used Process Excellence principles, problem-solving methodologies, and related tools when designing new systems and equipment or when starting a new and major business initiative. This resulted in competing "job jars" in which there were two sets of projects – those that mattered and those that did not. Process Excellence projects and studies were, unfortunately, in that latter category. Another way of relating this phenomenon is to realize that when an organization rewards fire fighting instead of fire prevention, the organization will tend to develop arsonists.

In conclusion, culture is a force that both supports and undermines most any effort related to meaningful change. Examine your organization's current culture and document its major attributes. Make a list of those that support meaningful change and those that are contrary to it. Leverage those that support change to garner earlier acceptance and address head-on those that will undermine change. And don't limit these discussions on culture to a one-time event. We suggest holding these at least annually as part of your Process Excellence assessments. Some of the reasons for gaps between actual and forecasted benefits will undoubtedly be related to cultural attributes. Peter Drucker, one of America's foremost management scientists who emphasized the need for employee partnership in Process Excellence, was reported to have said "culture eats change for breakfast." If so, then the right kind of change represents the nourishment needed to develop the culture being sought.

Change Management: Leveraging Cultural Strengths and Managing Its Weaknesses		
No.	Best Practice	Self-Assess Your Degree of Implementation (0-Min, 2-Max)
49.	View Process Excellence as a mindset, not just a toolset.	
50.	Leverage cultural strengths that promote change.	
Total (Max = 4):		

Table 10:
Checklist Summary for Chapter 10

Summary

Let's briefly return to our discussion about waste and its impact on realizing Process Excellence in our respective work places. We originally defined waste as any process, task, step, or activity that does not add or create value for the customer. When launching new products and services or performing major redesigns of existing ones, we defined waste as being those technical, organizational, and managerial impediments for preventing innovation from becoming truly systematic. If we challenged the creation or perpetuation of rigid systems, structures and processes that legitimize waste in the face of quality, speed, and cost, would we be better off? Are we demanding too much from senior management who must satisfy the markets and investors using near term results? Are we justified in exhorting people to work harder? Is much of our daily work accomplished by working on the wrong things? The answers to these and many other critically important questions are rooted in our efforts to "reverse the culture of waste."

This text represents a compendium of best practices for attaining Process Excellence. We return to the IPO diagram shown on the following page to emphasize a couple of key points. If we are to *realize* Process Excellence, we must be successful in improving the value delivered to our customers, the intellectual capital of our workforce, the growth of our organization, and the norms by which we operate. To achieve these ends, we need to deliver a continuum of innovative products and services that are better, faster, and less costly, all of which must occur through improved working relationships by those involved. This occurs through Process Excellence *implementation*. And to implement Process Excellence over time, we need to address each of the 10 elements illustrated as inputs on the left side of the IPO diagram.

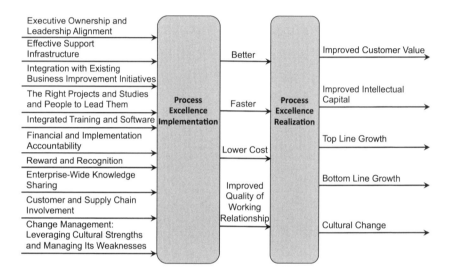

In close collaboration with our customers over the past 22 years, we have developed these 50 Best Practices described in this text and mapped them directly to these 10 inputs. These "Best Practices" represent the "how to's" for achieving excellence in the inputs. And if we are excellent on the inputs, the implementation and realization of Process Excellence will be successful. Given the context of your organization, be it a mature organization or a new startup, some of the best practices will resonate with you while others may not. Our hope is that these 50 Best Practices will provide valuable insights into your path ahead as you endeavor to reverse a "culture of waste" through Process Excellence.

Appendixes

- Appendix A – Master List of Best Practices

- Appendix B – Reader's Score Sheets and Percentile Table

- Appendix C – Key Process Excellence Infrastructure and Positions

	No.	Best Practice
Chapter 1 Executive Ownership and Leadership Alignment	1.	Establish ownership at the executive level.
	2.	Develop and communicate the need, vision, and plan.
	3.	Train leadership first.
	4.	Link compensation to involvement and success.
	5.	Continuously assess what is working and what is not and adjust.
Chapter 2 Effective Support Infrastructure	6.	Designate a well-respected Deployment Champion early.
	7.	Commission and use a guiding coalition.
	8.	Partner with a capable and reputable service provider.
	9.	Integrate key stakeholders into the plan.
	10.	Create position descriptions that mandate a pull for excellence.
	11.	Quickly attain a critical mass of practitioners.
Chapter 3 Integration with Existing Business Improvement Initiatives	12.	Maximize the synergy of multiple initiatives.
Chapter 4 The Right Projects and Studies and People to Lead Them	13.	Establish criteria for project selection and prioritization.
	14.	Use quick-hitting studies to accelerate results.
	15.	Select top-tier candidates for first waves of training.
Chapter 5 Integrated Training and Software	16.	Use motivational and experienced instructors and coaches.
	17.	Keep the software simple and easy to use.
	18.	Use a blended approach to learning.
Chapter 6 Financial and Implementation Accountability	19.	Use a consistent, simple and straightforward approach.
	20.	Generate successes early and communicate them.
	21.	Plan the service provider's exit strategy.
	22.	Develop internal subject matter experts.
	23.	Manage the expectations of every practitioner.
	24,	Define and use a meaty certification process.
	25.	Train all areas of the organization.
	26.	Apply the training immediately.
	27.	Provide expert coaching on all projects and studies.
	28.	Scope projects carefully.
	29.	Establish and follow rules for assessing benefits.

	No.	Best Practice
	30.	Publicize and use savings wisely.
	31.	Regularly review projects and act based on the assessment.
	32.	Conduct refresher sessions for leaders and practitioners.
	33.	Connect and use Champions to upgrade the initiative.
	34.	Make everyone aware of what is going on.
	35.	Design and use standardized templates.
	36.	Anticipate and manage position loss resulting from projects.
	37.	Include team-oriented "soft" tools.
	38.	Develop transfer functions to predict, optimize, and assess risk.
	39.	Make innovation systematic.
	40.	Solve new problems using trained resources and trumpet successes.
	41.	Make Process Excellence part of the human resource succession plan.
	42.	Integrate Process Excellence into all mergers and acquisitions.
	43.	Update the implementation plan based on feedback and results.
Chapter 7 Reward and Recognition	44.	Recognize people who execute successful projects.
	45.	Establish a project-tracking database and keep it current.
Chapter 8 Enterprise-Wide Knowledge Sharing	46.	Schedule benchmarking sessions.
	47.	Involve suppliers and customers early on.
Chapter 9 Customer and Supply Chain Involvement	48.	Implement a fact-based process for assessing the Voice of the Customer.
Chapter 10 Change Management: Leveraging Cultural Strengths and Managing Its Weaknesses	49.	View Process Excellence as a mindset, not just a toolset.
	50.	Leverage cultural strengths that promote change.

Enter the score from each of the 10 Chapter Tables in this score sheet and sum the 10 scores to get a Total Score.

Consolidated Process Excellence Score Sheet		
Input Variables (x's) ↓	Max Score	Insert Your Scores From Tables at End of Chapters 1-10 and Sum
Executive Ownership and Leadership Alignment (x_1)	10	
Effective Support Infrastructure (x_2)	12	
Integration with Existing Business Improvement Initiatives (x_3)	2	
The Right Projects and Studies and People to Lead Them (x_4)	6	
Integrated Training and Software (x_5)	6	
Financial and Implementation Accountability (x_6)	50	
Reward and Recognition (x_7)	2	
Enterprise-Wide Knowledge Sharing (x_8)	4	
Customer and Supply Chain Involvement (x_9)	4	
Change Management: Leveraging Cultural Strength and Managing Its Weaknesses (x_{10})	4	
Max Score & Your Total:	100	

Now locate your Total Score to the closest Total Score in the table below and note the corresponding percentile. This value allows you to compare your Total Score with 545 others who have also scored the 10 inputs. For example, if your Total Score is exactly 40, then your percentile is the 20th percentile, i.e., your score is as good as or better than 20% of the other 545 scores. It also means that 80% of the scores were higher than yours.

Total Score	Percentile	Total Score	Percentile
2	0%	52	39%
4	0%	54	43%
6	0%	56	45%
8	0%	58	48%
10	1%	60	52%
12	1%	62	56%
14	1%	64	59%
16	1%	66	62%
18	2%	68	65%
20	3%	70	70%
22	4%	72	72%
24	5%	74	77%
26	6%	76	81%
28	8%	78	85%
30	9%	80	88%
32	10%	82	90%
34	14%	84	93%
36	16%	86	95%
38	19%	88	97%
40	20%	90	98%
42	23%	92	99%
44	26%	94	100%
46	30%	96	100%
48	33%	98	100%
50	36%	100	100%

Additionally, you may be interested in doing a predictive analysis on how your scores impact the five output variables (or organizational performance measures) shown on the dual IPO diagram at the start of every chapter, namely:

- Customer Value
- Intellectual Capital
- Top Line Growth
- Bottom Line Growth
- Cultural Change

If you would like to see how your Best Practice scores impact these performance measures, visit www.airacad.com/predict. Be sure to take your 10 chapter scores from the above table with you to the site, because the predictive equations will need those 10 numbers in order to predict the values of the 5 outputs shown above. If you do that, you will then be able to compare your predictive performance scores with 545 others who have also rated the 10 inputs as well as the 5 outputs, and from whose data the prediction equations were generated. Performing such an analysis will allow you to see where your organization is strong and where it is weak with regard to the performance measures (compared to 545 others). Then you will also be able to examine the inputs (and thus the Best Practices) to see where improvements will have the biggest impact on the organizational performance measures. We highly recommend you try it. It is quick and easy to do and can be quite revealing.

Key Process Excellence Infrastructure and Positions

Position	Profile	Role	Training	Numbers
Process Excellence (PE) Steering Committee	• Composed of key operational executives on the corporation's leadership team. • Serves on a part-time basis in this capacity.	• Operationalizes, assesses and revitalizes the CEO/President's PE plan to maximize its benefits and relevancy to the business.	• Three day Champion training. • Periodic refresher training.	• One per the corporation.
Corporate or Business Unit Deployment Champion	• Senior, respected leader and mentor of business issues. • Line-of-sight reporting to CEO/president. • Strong proponent of PE who asks the right questions.	• Operationalizes the PE implementation plan; updates the leadership on its status including project and study status. • Manages the cadre of Champions and Belts. • Serves as the "eyes and ears" for the CEO/President on PE.	• Three day Champion training. • Periodic refresher training.	• One per the corporation and major business unit.
Project or RIE/Study Champion	• Senior, respected leader and mentor of business issues. • Strong proponent of PE who asks the right questions. • Serves as a business mentor for belts.	• Identifies projects/studies and aligns Belts with the projects. • Provides resources to accomplish project goals. • Breaks down barriers. • Promotes timely project/study completion and earlier benefit delivery.	• Three day Champion training. • Periodic refresher training.	• One per project or RIE/study.
Master Black Belt (Master)	• Technically excellent in the knowledge and application of lean and statistical tools. • Excellent communicator. • Respected Lean Six Sigma role model at all levels of the business.	• Technical mentor for Black Belts and Green Belts. • Internal consultant and trainer. • Generates breakthrough thinking for processes using Lean Six Sigma. • May serve on Lean Six Sigma Leadership Team.	• 1-2 weeks including Train-the-Trainer beyond Black Belt training.	• At least 1 per major business unit.
Black Belt (Expert)	• Respected by peers and management. • Master of basic through advanced tools. • Skilled in converting data into knowledge.	• Leads strategic, high impact process improvement projects and studies. • Change agent. • Teaches and mentors cross-functional team members and Green Belts. • Full-time project leader. • Converts gains into dollars.	• Four or five 1-week sessions with one month in between to apply the tools on projects and studies. • Project review in every session.	• 1 per 50 to 100 employees (1-2 %).
Green Belt (Specialist)	• Respected by peers. • Proficient in basic and intermediate tools. • Skilled in converting data into knowledge.	• Leads important process improvement teams. • Leads, trains and coaches on tools and analyses. • Assists Black Belts. • Typically serves part-time on projects.	• Two 1-week sessions with one month in between to apply the tools on projects and studies. • Project review in second session.	• 1 per 20 employees (5%).

List of Acronyms

CE	Cause & Effect
CMMI	Capability Maturity Model Integration
CNX	Controlled, Noise, eXperimental
CODN	Cost of Doing Nothing
COPQ	Cost of Poor Quality
COW	Cost of Waste
CTC	Critical - to - Customer
CTQ	Critical - to - Quality
DFSS	Design for Six Sigma
DMAIC	Define, Measure, Analyze, Improve, Control
DOE	Design of Experiments
DPMO	Defects Per Million Opportunities
5S	Sort, Set in order, Shine, Standardize, Sustain
FMEA	Failure Mode and Effects Analysis
FPY	First Pass Yield
IDOV	Identify, Design, Optimize, Validate
IPO	Input - Process – Output
KBM	Knowledge Based Management
KISS	Keep It Simple Statistically
LSS	Lean Six Sigma
MSA	Measurement System Analysis
NVA	Non-Value Added
PF	Process Flow
QCD	Quality, Cost, Delivery
QFD	Quality Function Deployment
ROI	Return on Investment
ROT	Rule of Thumb
RPN	Risk Priority Number
RTY	Rolled Throughput Yield
SIPOC	Supplier-Input-Process-Output-Customer
SOP	Standard Operating Procedure
VA	Value Added
VOC	Voice of Customer
VOP	Voice of Process

Glossary

Benchmarking: An activity that encompasses the search for and implementation of best practices.

Best Practice: A generally accepted, informally standardized technique, method, or process that has proven itself over time to accomplish given tasks. It represents a standard way of doing things that multiple organizations can and should use.

Black Belt: A key person who is trained to execute critical projects and deliver breakthrough enhancements to the bottom line; also known as an expert or change agent.

Bottom Line Growth: Refers to an increase, over time, of a company's net income.

Breakthrough Improvement: An order-of-magnitude positive change in the way an organization operates. This may involve the introduction of new technology, a change in culture or structure, or adopting/developing a new system or process. This definition is analogous to the Japanese term "Kaikaku" implying the radical overhaul of an activity to eliminate waste (muda in Japanese).

Business Process Management: A management approach focused on aligning all aspects of a company with the wants and needs of its customers. It promotes business effectiveness and efficiency, continuous process improvement, innovation, flexibility, and technology.

Certification: Refers to the confirmation of certain characteristics of an object, person, or organization. In the context of Process Excellence, it demonstrates an individual's mastery in the terminology, methodologies, and tools associated with Process Excellence as applied to important projects and studies that deliver continuous and/or breakthrough improvements. The steps toward certification generally consist of training, completion of a written exam, project and study work that yield documented benefits back to the sponsoring organization, and successful oral presentations and written reports of the projects and studies to executive management.

Champion: A leader or manager who is a strong advocate of Process Excellence and who serves as a Deployment Leader or project sponsor or process owner within the Process Excellence rollout.

Coaching (or Mentoring): The practice of supporting an individual through a process of achieving a specific personal or professional result. In Process Excellence, coaching is often provided to a Deployment or Project Champion as well as to Belts, Experts, or Agents in order to complete their assigned tasks in a timely and effective manner for benefit realization.

Competitive Excellence: A term used to describe a state of competence of an organization; it means the organization has the ability to survive the current demands of the marketplace and evolve itself to a state of continued and expanded success. It also refers to the initiative of pursuing this state of excellence through a knowledge based strategy, synchronizing the business and embracing its intellectual capital using the best of the best improvement methods.

Conjoint Analysis: A marketing term that refers to a statistical technique requiring research participants to make a series of trade-offs in order to reveal the relative importance of component attributes. To improve the predictability of the analysis, survey participants should be grouped into similar segments based on objectives, values and/or other factors.

Continuous Improvement (CI): Refers to an ongoing effort to improve products, services, and processes primarily through incremental improvement over time versus "breakthrough" or order-of-magnitude change all at once. A vehicle for implementing CI is the Kaizen event.

Cost of Poor Quality (COPQ): The cost of the "waste" associated with all of the processes (administrative and production oriented) within a business. This includes costs related to internal and external failures, appraisal, prevention and lost opportunities. Often associated with any activity related to not doing the right things right the first time.

Critical to Customer (CTC): A measure of process or product performance that is related to customer requirements or customer satisfaction; it is usually associated with timeliness (speed), quality (accuracy), or cost; a CTC must be measurable. Also referred to as a CTQ or Critical to Quality.

Culture: The values and behaviors that contribute to the unique social and psychological environment of an organization. The sum of an organization's past and current assumptions, experiences, philosophy, and values that hold it together, and is expressed in its self-image, inner workings, interactions with the outside world and future expectations.

Customer: Anyone who directly or indirectly uses or consumes a product or service, whether internal or external to the providing organization or provider.

Customer Needs and Expectations: Customer wants, desires, wishes and demands for products and services translated into measurable indicators of cost, quality (various dimensions), and delivery (time and quantity). Often referred to as customer requirements.

Cycle Time: How long it takes a process, as timed by observation, to complete a part, product, or service. This time includes operating time, waiting time, and the time required to prepare, load, and unload.

De-Scope: In the context of Process Excellence, it refers to reducing the time to complete a project by narrowing the project's latitude (boundaries), including the number of resources required to work on the desired improvement. De-scoping typically occurs when the project contract is being formulated as well as during the Define and Measure phases of DMAIC.

Design for Six Sigma (DFSS): An improvement strategy that is particularly useful during the early phases of the product or service development cycle with the intention of reducing variability and "designing the quality in" rather than improving the process or product later.

Design of Experiments (DOE): An organized method of collecting data by purposefully changing the process inputs in order to observe and measure the corresponding changes in the process output. DOE provides a method to evaluate input factors independently and develop powerful empirical models that approximate the true relationships between various process inputs and the output. Understanding these relationships allows us to improve and optimize the process performance characteristics.

DFLSS: Design for Lean Six Sigma. As used herein, a variant of DFSS.

DFSS Scorecard: The repository of the cumulative body of knowledge regarding a design of a product or service. It is broken down into segments such as parts, process, performance and software. It is a living document that reflects the current state of the design and predicted capability.

DMAIC: Define > Measure > Analyze > Improve > Control is the standard Six Sigma and Lean Six Sigma phase gate process for project execution.

EBITDA: A company's earnings before interest, taxes, depreciation, and amortization. It is often used in parallel with or as an alternative to the price-to-earnings (P/E) ratio.

E-learning: E-learning comprises all forms of electronically supported learning and teaching. The information and communication systems, whether networked or not, serve as specific media to implement the learning process.

Evolution: The competitive excellence domain focused on the development of new products and services; the ability of an organization to recreate itself by developing new life cycle curves. It is driven by the Voice of Society or societal needs.

Executive Advocacy: Full knowledge and acceptance of the responsibility and accountability for the Process Excellence rollout by the President/CEO through actions and communication.

Failure Mode and Effects Analysis (FMEA): A tool which is used to systematically identify, analyze, prioritize (on the basis of a risk assessment) and reduce or eliminate potential process or product failure modes.

Functional Analysis System Technique (FAST): A design technique used to define the functions of a system, subsystem, or component in terms of "how" functions are accomplished and "why" functions are used. These link together to show the overall functionality of the system, subsystem, or component for subsequent engineering development. It links very nicely with FMEA.

Green Belt: A person trained to undertake DMAIC projects or studies in his own job function and/or to provide technical assistance to a Black Belt on a more expansive project; also known as a specialist or associate.

IDOV: Identify > Design > Optimize > Validate is the original DFSS phased gate process for executing projects in new product or process development.

Infrastructure: In the context of Process Excellence, those deployment and project/study Champions and Belts, Agents, etc., along with the organizational support structure, which are required to design, implement, and sustain the rollout over time.

Innovation: The act of discovering and introducing something new or creative that satisfies a societal need.

Input-Process-Output (IPO) Diagram: A visual representation of a process where inputs are represented by input arrows to a box (which represents the process) and outputs are shown using arrows emanating out of the box.

Intellectual Capital: The value that the employees of a business provide through the application of skills, know-how, and expertise. The intellectual capital of an organization is significantly enhanced through the teaching and proper application of Process Excellence tools and methodologies for the purpose of solving relevant business problems and attaining competency to solve increasingly difficult problems.

Kaizen: Continuous small (incremental) improvements in an activity over time which reduce waste.

KISS: Keep It Simple Statistically. Also, Keeping Innovation Structured and Systematic.

Knowledge Based Management (KBM): A leadership and management philosophy predicated on good decision making which emphasizes the use of knowledge and data rather than opinion and perception. It is composed of three elements: the Questions Leaders Need to Answer, Questions Leaders Need to Ask, and the improvement strategies described in the KBM Text that are needed to generate and deliver the right knowledge to the right people at the right time.

Kotter's Change Model: An eight-step model that organizations need to implement to successfully change a culture. A Harvard professor, John Kotter is regarded as an authority on leadership and change. His eight steps are:

- Create a sense of urgency.
- Develop a guiding coalition.
- Develop a vision for change.
- Communicate the vision.
- Empower broad-based action.
- Generate short-term wins.
- Don't let up.
- Make it stick in the organizational culture.

Lean: The continuous elimination of unnecessary, non-value added steps (or waste) within a process or value stream. It is also an improvement strategy that embraces two primary principles, flow and pull, for the purpose of removing waste.

Lean Six Sigma: A business philosophy and improvement strategy that combines the strategies of Lean (reduction of waste and queue times) and Six Sigma (reduction of variation). These concepts must be applied to all facets of the business in order to achieve a truly "lean enterprise."

Master Black Belt: A full-time resource who is both a technical mentor for Black Belts and Green Belts and also an internal consultant and trainer.

Mentoring (or Coaching): The practice of supporting an individual through a process of achieving a specific personal or professional result. In Process Excellence, mentoring is often provided to a Deployment or Project Champion as well as to Belts, Experts, or Agents in order to complete their assigned tasks in a timely and effective manner for benefit realization.

Metric: A performance measure that is considered to be a key pulse point of an organization. It should be aligned to goals or objectives and carefully monitored.

Mission: Defines the fundamental purpose of an organization or an enterprise, succinctly describing why it exists and what it does to achieve its vision. It is sometimes used to set out a "picture" of the organization in the future. A mission statement provides details of what is done and answers the question: "What do we do?"

Needs: Those essential and specific actions, tasks, or activities that must be undertaken by the organization to implement its strategic plan. "Needs" also refers to the unwritten or unspoken requirements of a customer.

Non-Value Added (NVA): Activities that consume time or resources but do not directly contribute toward meeting the customer's requirements.

OPEX: Acronym for "Operational Excellence." It is synonymous with Competitive Excellence, Process Excellence, Lean Six Sigma, etc.

Oregon Productivity Matrix (OPM): A method for indexing performance measures and calculating a combined multi-factor performance index. It is an objective matrix developed by the University of Oregon for identifying, analyzing, and tracking critical metrics relevant to the strategic decision making process.

Output: A product produced or a service delivered by a process. More specifically, it is a measure of a product or service that is typically associated with cost, quality/accuracy, and delivery (time and quantity).

Over-processing: The waste that occurs when more work is done on a part, product, or service than what is required by the customer. This also includes using tools that are more precise, complex, or expensive than absolutely required.

Paradigm: A set of boundaries (perhaps consciously, subconsciously, or even unconsciously defined) that form the limits of behavior, opinions, and decision-making.

PEM: Psychological and Emotional Methods of creativity – the collection of general innovation techniques that produces a host of ideas (i.e., a divergent process).

PF/CE/CNX/SOP: A management philosophy and methodology, as well as a Rapid Improvement Event, which is used to reduce extraneous waste and variation. It uses Process Flow (PF) diagrams and Cause and Effect (CE) diagrams to identify and sort the causes of waste and variation. The causes are further categorized as Controllable ("C"), Noise ("N") or eXperimental ("X"). Standard operating procedures (SOPs) are used to change as many "N" factors into "C" factors as possible.

Position Description: A document describing duties, supervisory controls, and responsibilities for a particular position. It classifies those elements and establishes pay schedule, job title, series, grade, and competitive level. A position description may describe more than one position.

Predictor variables (x's): The independent variables or factors that influence an outcome or response. These are the inputs associated with the arrows leading into an Input-Process-Output diagram.

Preservation: The competitive excellence domain that focuses on maintaining or protecting the current market position of a business; it includes maintaining market share, profitability, and brand recognition. It is driven by the voice of the customer (VOC).

Process: An activity which blends a set of inputs for the purpose of producing a product, providing a service, or performing a task.

Process Excellence: Represents those activities specifically designed to create excellent processes in terms of speed, quality, and cost. These activities include the terminology, tools, methodologies, and best practices contained within this text and its sister text entitled *Knowledge Based Management* (KBM).

Project: Refers to the work effort required to successfully complete the entire set of phases or tollgates in executing the LSS (DMAIC) or DFSS (IDOV) methodology.

Project Scope: Includes the project's deliverables, boundaries, and requirements. These are identified as part of a project contract that should be in place before the first week of Process Excellence-related training. It should be re-visited at the first sign of scope creep or project delay.

Proof of Competency: A real and demonstrated ability to successfully carry out some activity that is well defined. Demonstrating the ability to reliably and predictably solve relevant business problems using the associated terminology, methodologies, and tools is a major requirement for Process Excellence Belts, Experts, or Agents to achieve certification.

Proof of Concept: The demonstration of feasibility of some concept, method, or process. Proof of Concept is achieved in Process Excellence when an initial set of projects and studies are commissioned and successfully completed.

Quality Function Deployment (QFD): A systematic process used to integrate customer requirements into every aspect of the design and delivery of products and services.

Rapid Improvement Event (RIE): A quick-hitting improvement effort that should not last longer than five days. Within a LSS (DMAIC) project, it is usually part of the Improve phase. Also known as a Kaizen event or a PF/CE/CNX/SOP event.

Response Variable (y): The dependent or response variables of a process. These variables are associated with the arrows leading out of the IPO diagram.

Return on Investment (ROI): A metric that is used to gauge the overall success of a Process Excellence initiative, or the success of individual projects and studies conducted within the improvement strategy. The financial savings are usually measured as a percentage of the original financial investment or, if on an annual basis, as a percentage of the revenue or budget.

Self-Sustainability: The state of an organization that allows it to design, implement, sustain, and revitalize its Process Excellence initiative without the need for external experts or consultants, while still maintaining the same or higher level of benefits.

Sigma: A Greek letter (σ) used to represent the standard deviation of a population of data. It is a measure of variation of a data set.

Single Piece Flow: A production strategy in which units progress individually (as a batch of one unit) through each of its associated process steps with continuous flow in the forward direction (i.e., without rework). It can be contrasted with the batch and queue strategy in which batches of multiple units proceed as a group through each of the production steps. This procedure requires each unit to "stop and wait" for each of the other units in the batch to be completed before the group proceeds to the next process step.

Six Sigma: A performance improvement and business strategy that began in the 1980's at Motorola. Emphasis is on reducing defects, reducing cycle time with aggressive goals, and reducing costs to dramatically impact the bottom line. It involves establishing an organizational infrastructure together with a repeatable methodology and tools to accomplish business objectives.

Societal Needs (Voice of Society): These are the drivers for new product development, because customers will not be able to relate what they will need or want just a few years downstream.

Standard Operating Procedures (SOPs): An up-to-date written procedure that clearly and concisely describes the exact method to be followed in order to complete a specific task.

Steering Committee: An advisory committee usually made up of high level stakeholders and/or experts who provide guidance on key issues such as company policy and objectives, budgetary control, marketing strategy, resource allocation, and decisions involving large expenditures. A Process Excellence steering committee formulates the Process Excellence implementation plan and assesses its implementation over time with emphasis on project execution, resource allocation, and benefit realization.

Study: An effort that is smaller in scope than a project. A study is the application of a tool or methodology that provides immediate knowledge for the purpose of gaining quick successes. A study does not complete the entire tollgate phases of DMAIC or IDOV. Multiple studies are typically needed to complete a DMAIC or IDOV project.

Succession Planning: Represents a process for identifying and developing internal people with the potential to fill key leadership positions in the company. Succession planning increases the availability of experienced and capable employees that are prepared to assume these roles as they become available. Successful certified Belts, Experts, or Change Agents merit consideration in their organization's succession plan.

Survey: A means of gathering data on people, processes, products, and organizations. It is usually accomplished via questionnaires, interviews, etc.

SWOT: Strengths, weaknesses, opportunities, and threats.

Synergistic: The interaction or cooperation of two or more organizations, substances, agents, or factors to produce a combined effect greater than the sum of their separate effects. Lean (e.g., faster and less expensive) and Six Sigma (e.g., better and less expensive) are highly synergistic since their combined application (Lean Six Sigma) yields better products and services delivered faster at lower cost.

Systematic Change: A non-random, sustainable change. In the context of Process Excellence, this would represent a long-term change in an organization's products, services, processes, technology, and culture triggered, at least in part, by a change in its strategic or business plan.

Systematic Improvement: Improvement that is planned, repeatable, and predictable over time and involves broad cross-sections of the workforce, if not the entire workforce, in the organization.

Top Line Growth: Refers to the expansion over time of a company's gross sales or revenues.

Transfer Function: This is a mathematical relationship between a response variable (y) and one or more input or predicator variables (x's).

TRIZ: In Russian, Teoriya Resheniya Izobretatelskikh Zadatch, which translated into English means Theory of Inventive Problem Solving. Developed by Genrich Altshuller, TRIZ is an innovative problem solving methodology that converges on the solution(s) rather than promoting divergent thought processes for innovation.

Value: Some feature, condition, service, or product that the customer considers desirable and is willing to pay for.

Value Stream: All of the activities that are performed to transform a product or service into what is required by the customer.

Variability: A generic term that refers to the property of a metric (or key measurement) to take on different values.

Vision: Ideals, hopes, and dreams that bring meaning to what we do. It provides the reason for an organization's being.

Voice of the Customer (VOC): A term that describes any method of collecting information about what is important to the customer. It includes but is not limited to: customer specifications, customer design requirements, customer surveys, and listening to customer feedback. When capability is computed, VOC is represented by specifications.

Waste: Any activity or process that, from the perspective of the customer, does not add value to the product or service.

WIIFM principle: Acronym for "What's in it for me."

Index